*Praise for*
# HOW AND HOW NOT TO BE HAPPY

"There is simply no more powerful, profound, or persuasive Christian writer on controversial themes alive in the world today than J. Budziszewski. Just reading this brilliantly written book will make you happy. Living it will be even more potent."
　　**—Peter Kreeft,** professor of philosophy at Boston College
　　and author of *A Summa of the Summa*

"Budziszewski has written a fascinating and sublimely readable book. Many authors have taken up this theme, and many have managed to be boring or even vapid, despite the intrinsic interest of the question. With his razor-sharp power of cutting through fallacies, and his extraordinary ability to come up with just the right examples from his treasury of experience, Budziszewski has produced the best book on happiness that you are ever going to read. Rightly understood, happiness is available!"
　　**—Matthew Levering,** James N. and Mary D. Perry Jr. Chair
　　of Theology, Mundelein Seminary

"Budziszewski is certainly on the side of the angels, and I find his theological work of high quality (especially for a philosopher who specializes in politics usually). He has been heroic in his writing about chastity. He also gets the broader (i.e., societal and personal) implications of what theologians commonly teach about the place of the real good in the moral life. This is a readable book that everyone can learn from about the one thing that matters: happiness."
　　**—Romanus Cessario,** O.P., Adam Cardinal Maida Professor
　　of Theology, Ave Maria University

"J. Budziszewski unites a deep expertise in the most important thinking about happiness with an intimate familiarity with our current crisis in seeking happiness. *How and How Not to be Happy* responds to contemporary difficulties, incorporates modern perspectives, and re-presents in a new and fresh way perennial insights from classic thinkers about the true nature of human flourishing. Students, professors, and intelligent readers can gain great profit and pleasure from reading this book."

—**Christopher Kaczor,** author of *The Gospel of Happiness: How Secular Psychology Points to the Wisdom of Christian Practice* and co-author of *Jordan Peterson, God, and Christianity: The Search for a Meaningful Life*

"Rare is the book that so easily combines deep, interdisciplinary thinking about happiness with an accessible and often beguiling conversational tone that will draw in every reader. Too often, books on happiness are either thick philosophy or glib pop psychology, but Professor Budziszewski succeeds admirably in drawing on and purifying the wisdom of both the philosophical and psychological traditions to provide a real feast for those who want to get beyond 'easy answers and instead seek to be 'deconfused' about this most important topic."

—**David Cloutier,** associate professor of philosophy at the Catholic University of America

"There is much talk about happiness today, but not much wisdom about it. Yet that is precisely what the greatest philosophers of the Western tradition, and especially Aristotle and Aquinas, have to offer us. There is a desperate need to make that wisdom available beyond the ivory tower, to the general public. J. Budziszewski does the job with his usual clarity, erudition, and good sense."

—**Edward Feser,** professor of philosophy at Pasadena City College

"Everyone, Aristotle observed, wants to be happy. But what is happiness, and how do we achieve it? There, he noted, 'the many do not give the same account as the wise.' It's hard to think of anyone who approaches the question with greater wisdom than J. Budziszewski. This book overflows with subtlety, insight, and a profound understanding of what it is to be human. An education in arts and letters all by itself, it combines philosophical depth with practical advice on how to avoid the snares that catch all of us some of the time and many of us most of the time. And it's a pleasure to read. If you want to be happier, more fulfilled, and understand more about who and what you are, you need this book."

> —**Daniel A. Bonevac,** professor of philosophy at the University of Texas at Austin

"People who know what true happiness is (and there is an answer) won't need this book. Those who don't know, also won't know that they need this book and need to buy it. The obvious answer is for those who don't need this book to buy it, to give as a gift for those who do. One could hardly find a truer act of love."

> —**Michael Pakaluk,** professor of ethics and social philosophy at the Catholic University of America and author of *Mary's Voice in the Gospel according to John*

"We all want happiness, but yet it seems so elusive. In this wonderful little book, J. Budziszewski explains why. Relying on the insights of ancient wisdom, he takes us through all the dead ends that we mistake for happiness. He even shows us why some modern attempts (by Jonathan Haidt and others) to tap into that wisdom fail because they dismiss or ignore the transcendent source to which it points. In an age of ever-increasing distractions and banal amusements, all of us, especially young people, need some direction on the meaning and acquisition of happiness. I can't think of a better guide than this book."

> —**Francis J. Beckwith,** professor of philosophy and church-state studies at Baylor University

# How and How Not to be Happy

# How *and* How Not *to be* Happy

## J. Budziszewski

REGNERY GATEWAY
Washington, D.C.

Regnery Gateway™ is a trademark of Salem Communications Holding Corporation
Regnery® is a registered trademark and its colophon is a trademark of Salem Communications Holding Corporation

Cataloging-in-Publication data on file with the Library of Congress

ISBN: 978-1-68451-107-5
eISBN: 978-1-68451-290-4
Library of Congress Control Number: 2021946365

Published in the United States by
Regnery Gateway
An Imprint of Regnery Publishing
A Division of Salem Media Group
Washington, D.C.
www.RegneryGateway.com

Manufactured in the United States of America

10 9 8 7 6 5 4 3 2 1

Books are available in quantity for promotional or premium use. For information on discounts and terms, please visit our website: www.RegneryGateway.com.

To Sandra
*She openeth her mouth with wisdom;*
*and in her tongue is the law of kindness.*

# Contents

# *Preface*

"Man's mind seeks to recover its proper good...but, like a drunken man knows not by what path to return home."[1]

This little book is about a very large topic: human happiness. Why write about it at all? Not for a moment do I think we are ignorant about this subject—though I do think we are confused about a great deal of what we half-know about it. The purpose of this book might be described as *deconfusing* some of our inherited semi-knowledge.

If you are the sort of person who likes to cut right to the chase, you may want to skip right now to Part Two, because this preface and the first few chapters aren't about happiness itself—they are about preliminaries like why happiness needs to be studied, how to study it, and why I've written this book the way I have. After all, if you start wondering about those questions later on, you can always backtrack. People like me, though, who are always asking, "Why did you conduct your investigation *that* way instead of *this* way?" will prefer not to skip anything and read straight through. It's up to you.

A great deal of what has been written on the topic of happiness amounts to stating its necessary conditions: things the absence of which will make you *unhappy*. It seems to me that these necessary conditions are pretty obvious. The interesting thing is the *sufficient* conditions of happiness: things the presence of which will make you happy. Are there any things like that? For example, I know that if I have no friends I will be unhappy—but does having friends guarantee that I will be happy?

I am not trying to prove anything, if by proof we mean something that will convince any sane person as a matter of sheer logic. The sorts of arguments that I make are what philosophers call "probable." In other words, I try to give good reasons for accepting my conclusions—the best reasons I know of, usually appealing to other things we already accept.

The book is succinct; some might say terse. I can treat large matters fairly quickly because a very long tradition of probable arguments lies in the background, allowing me to ride piggyback on other thinkers. The book isn't as terse as what I consider to be the greatest of all treatments of the subject, the *Treatise on Happiness and Ultimate Purpose*, written by Thomas Aquinas in the late thirteenth century. His *Treatise*—a single section of a much longer work[2]—is so fast-moving and densely packed that in the original language it is only a little more than one-third the length of this one, and even so covers more ground. I couldn't have written this little book unless I had first written a very long one, 653 pages of line-by-line commentary[3] on that very short one by St. Thomas—and I would never presume to compare what I present here to the master's treatise. But despite the great deal that I have learned from him (and my debt will be obvious to those who know his work), in this book I am speaking for myself; it is not in any way meant to substitute for his.

Although I don't think this book is difficult, it is not a "Made Easy" or "For Dummies" book either. Any author who claims to present "Four Simple Steps to Total Happiness" or "Seven Days to Change Your Life" is a liar. It would be surprising, wouldn't it, if there really were four steps to happiness, or seven, or three, that had never before been discovered in all the previous centuries of human living? I wouldn't believe anyone who made such claims. Obviously, though, millions do. Just look at the bestseller lists.

What else might you wish to know about this book before you dig in? Perhaps I should offer a little warning. While preparing it, I came across a review of a book I had consulted about the psychology of self-esteem. One of the reviewer's complaints was that the author of the book made "frequent use of the detritus of popular media." If you share the reviewer's snobbery, then my book will annoy you, because when I need to illustrate matters that cannot be easily counted and correlated, I too make use of such "detritus." The funny thing is that in his own book, the reviewer also illustrated points with pop culture references, though he labored to distinguish the way *he* used them, which he viewed as sophisticated and scientifically grown-up, with the way the other author used them, which he saw as slumming.

Ironically, the great thinkers and writers of the past didn't hesitate to use popular illustrations. For instance, to illustrate a point about his famous doctrine of the mean, Aristotle contrasts the amount of food an athletic novice needs to eat with the amount that the famous wrestler Milo of Croton needs to eat.[4] If using Milo to illustrate is slumming, then so be it. I'm with Aristotle.

Before taking a chance on this book, you may also want to know my attitude toward statistics. I do use them, but sparingly, and with a grain of salt. The human mind is an extraordinary instrument for synthesizing diverse sorts of experiences. Though it makes mistakes, it is able to come to conclusions that are far ahead of what the numerical tabulation of things has shown or is ever likely to show; and the notion that statistics can tell us everything we need to know is pure fantasy. Fetishizing numbers doesn't make the study of human beings more rigorous and scientific, but less. One year I was teaching my students one of the classics of American social philosophy, Alexis de Tocqueville's *Democracy in America*, which is now almost two centuries old. Tocqueville was a keen observer and a subtle student of human nature who drew innumerable connections among all sorts of things the rest of us may have half-noticed about ourselves but never paused to think about. With some of the students, though—I am glad to say only a few of them—Tocqueville's wisdom cut no ice. Having taken too strong a dose of social science pills, they demanded, "Where is his survey data?" Just because he did not provide correlations and regressions in the modern style, they refused to consider whether any of Tocqueville's observations might have been true. It astonished me: they were not even willing to make use of their own everyday experience.

If ostentatiously waved numbers sometimes impress us more than they should, the problem is usually that the writer waving them around is assuming away the answers to the hardest questions, asking only the easy ones. Rather than looking deeply into what happiness is, for example, he may take for granted without thinking about it that happiness must be a feeling and that people always know how they are feeling—so that to understand happiness all we have to do is ask people what makes them feel good and then crunch the survey numbers. But what if happiness isn't a feeling in the first place?

Statistics can be useful for finding out some things. If one can confirm statistically, for example, that children who are praised for everything they do are more likely than other children to have inflated opinions of themselves, well and good. On the other hand, maybe we don't need factor analysis or logistic regression to know that! Some empiricists think that philosophy is merely poor sociology. I think that's backwards. With all respect to some fine sociologists whom I number among my friends, a good deal of sociology is really just bad philosophy.

So though from time to time I do mention helpful statistics—and I am truly and humbly grateful to have them—statistics are not useful except to a person who already knows *something*. It would be lunacy to demand statistical proof that we come in two sexes, that we differ from the beasts, or that we wonder about the meaning of things. My purpose is to put everyday observations about things that we already know something about into better order than we usually put them, so that the dim and disconnected outlines of what we know can become sharper.

Thus, despite the common confusion and inconsistency of what passes for common sense, I am not one of its despisers; the thing to do with common sense is purify and elevate it. If now and then this book unearths or clarifies a few things that we tend not to notice until they are called to our attention, I will count myself satisfied.

Nothing more remains to be done in this preface but a bit of housekeeping.

From time to time I have adapted and modified a sentence or a paragraph from some other book I have written, because it can be hard to find better language for something that one has striven to say well before. I am grateful to the publishers of my previous books for permission to do so. Needless to say, I hope my readers will read those other books too.[5]

I have tried not to weigh the book down with excessive notes. In cases in which my notes don't give page numbers, the reason is either that I am citing an old book available in many editions or that I am using an unpaginated electronic source. When I can, I give other pointers such as chapter numbers.

For the convenience of readers, I have preferred to use translations that are in the public domain, and for books and translations in the public domain I don't usually give publication information, though I do usually give the names of translators. Generally speaking, I give quotations in the original language only when they have passed over into proverbs that are usually quoted that way.

I think that's all. Happy reading! And I do mean *happy*.

# PART ONE

## Getting Started

"What a chaos, what a subject of contradiction,
what a prodigy!"[1]

# CHAPTER 1

# Why Is How to Be Happy or Fulfilled Even a Question?

"On countless occasions I have made abundant speeches...
and very good speeches they were, so I thought—but now
I cannot say one word as to what it is."[1]

A re people happy? It's difficult to know even whether they think they are. The 2017 Harris Poll Survey of American Happiness reported low numbers (33 percent) of people calling themselves "happy."[2] But the 2020 Gallup Poll reported that very high numbers of people were "satisfied with their personal life" (about 90 percent).[3] This isn't because people suddenly became happier during those three years; the Gallup percentage was almost as high in 2017 as in 2020. It's because of how the question was asked.

We aren't going to learn much from such numbers. My own suspicion is that although most people have some share in happiness, not many are simply happy. But for now, let's simply ask how happiness is attained.

There are two kinds of people in the world: those who say there are two kinds of people in the world, and... all right, there are more than two. But we can sort those who want to know how to be happy, from those who say we shouldn't ask.

By far the greater number of people belong to the group who wants to know. It seems obvious to them that happiness is not only good but *the great good*. It also seems clear to them not just that we all ought to pursue it, but that we all do pursue it. The authors of the Declaration of Independence regarded the pursuit of happiness as so important that they called it an unalienable right, right up there with life and liberty.

If you aren't sure whether people desire happiness, then ask them a few simple questions. When we act deliberately, do we act for the sake of some good? Sure. I brush my teeth so that they won't become diseased and fall out. When we act for the sake of some good, do we sometimes pursue that good for the sake of some further good? Of course. I pursue the good of healthy teeth because if I lost my teeth it would be difficult to eat and speak. Now comes the clincher. Does this chain ever come to an end—is there some good or set of goods for the sake of which we seek other goods, but which we seek for its own sake?

As Aristotle discovered, the vast majority of people reply yes.[4] We call this good or set of goods "happiness"—or an equivalent term, such as "thriving," "flourishing," "satisfaction," or "fulfillment." People have agreed on this in pretty much every place and time. Though people disagree about what happiness is, they are rarely in doubt that it is their ultimate desire. Whatever it is to be fulfilled, they want to be fulfilled. Whatever it is to flourish, they want to flourish. This book is for them.

What about the minority who say that we shouldn't ask how to be happy? This book is for them too, because I would like to ask them to rethink.

Consider Rafael Euba, a psychiatrist affiliated with King's College, London, who urges, "Humans Aren't Designed to Be Happy—So Stop Trying." According to Euba, "We should take comfort in the knowledge that unhappiness is not really our fault. It is the fault of our natural design. It is in our blueprint."

How is it in our blueprint? "Humans are not designed to be happy, or even content," he argues. "Instead, we are designed primarily to survive and reproduce, like every other creature in the natural world. A state of contentment is discouraged by nature because it would lower our guard against possible threats to our survival." (I wonder why nature didn't just wire us so that contentment didn't lower our guard?) In some cases even depression can be good, Euba explains, "by helping the depressed individual disengage from risky and hopeless situations in which he or she cannot win." He writes, "If you are unhappy at times, this is not a shortcoming that demands urgent repair, as the happiness gurus would have it." In fact, "pretending that any degree of pain is abnormal or pathological will only foster feelings of inadequacy and frustration."[5]

Notice the inconsistencies in Dr. Euba's account. Though he says we aren't made to be "content," yet he says we can "take comfort" in knowing that this is so. Taking comfort sounds a lot like seeking contentment. He argues that we should "stop trying" to be happy because we aren't made for it, yet he says we are meant to "seek gratification" and "avoid pain." Pursuing gratification and avoiding pain sure sound as though they have something to do with happiness.

And what does it mean to say that unhappiness can sometimes do us good? Doesn't it mean that unhappiness in the short run can help make us happier in the long run?

So stripping his prose of its exaggerations, dissonances, and curtsies toward Darwin, not even Dr. Euba really denies that happiness is attainable. In fact, he thinks we are designed to seek such happiness as we can reach. What he denies is that *abiding* happiness is reachable. And why is it so important not to expect abiding happiness? Because wanting it will make us unhappy!

This bundle of inconsistencies raises an interesting question to which we will return. On Dr. Euba's theory, no deep longing should exist in our minds unless it is adaptive. Now it would be maladaptive to long for things that are impossible. We desire to satisfy our hunger and thirst, to survive dangers, to have children, and to quench the pains of desire for the things of this world, and such longings make sense because they are for possible things. By this reasoning, if abiding happiness is impossible, then the longing for it should not exist at all. Any such desire should have died out over the course of evolution. Like "every other creature in the natural world," we should be completely satisfied with transitory relief: This meal. This sleep. This scratching of this itch. This escape from pursuit, and this coupling with this female. We should approach everything in life the way the hookup culture approaches sex.

Yet we do long for abiding happiness. In fact, the yearning for this "abstract idea with no equivalent in actual human experience," as Dr. Euba calls it, is so strong that he finds it necessary to warn us sternly against heeding it. Ignore that seducer! he urges. Resist that temptation! Pay no attention to the man behind the curtain!

Why? Surely the longing for happiness itself is a constant of "actual human experience," one of the things that *separates* the nature of the rational animal from "every other creature in the natural world." But of course, if we start thinking that happiness is possible, we will no longer be able to blame evolution if the way that we live is immiserating us.

And yet Dr. Euba is right to warn against the snake-oil sellers and the peddlers of nostrums, the gurus who teach that we can float through earthly life in a cloud of bliss, in a continuous *up* with no *downs*. Whatever abiding happiness is, it isn't *that*.

Dr. Euba's reasons are not the only ones people give for declining to ask how to be happy. Let's consider a few of the other objections, because there is something to each of them—as there is something to his. There would have to be, for if there were nothing to them at all, then no one at all could believe them. There is some grain of truth in everything a human being finds plausible. That doesn't mean that it expresses the whole truth and expresses it well; it doesn't even mean that it expresses a lot of it. The trick is to unravel what it does get right from what it doesn't. Which is pretty much the method of this book.

One objection is that those who are always asking, "How can I be happy?" are the very ones least likely to be happy. There are two things right about this objection. The first is that the ascent to happiness doesn't lie through the valley of obsession, whether the obsession concerns happiness or anything else. But notice that a person who points this out isn't really saying that we don't need to know about happiness. He is claiming that he *already* knows something about it—he knows that we won't attain it by obsessing over it! And this is true. It's one thing to say that we shouldn't obsess about happiness, and another to say that we shouldn't inquire into it at all. In fact, if the objector hadn't already looked into the matter, then *how could he know* that obsession isn't helpful? But if this is the *only* thing he knows about happiness, then he needs to take his inquiry further.

The person who warns against asking, "How can I be happy?" may also be making a true observation—not about happiness, but about pleasure. Most people do confuse pleasure with happiness—a confusion I take up later on. The objector may be making the point that those who make pleasure the goal of all their actions find that pleasure slips from their grasp. And this is also true. For example, I gain the pleasure of friendship by focusing on friendship, not by focusing on pleasure; if I am always thinking, "How much pleasure am I getting from this?" then I miss the whole point of the friendship—and so I lose its pleasure too. We need to ask *what* happiness has to do with pleasure—and with friendship—and with many other things.

A second objection is that seeking happiness is selfish, because we ought to seek other people's happiness. What is right about this objection is that I shouldn't take the attitude, "Every man for himself." What is mistaken is the idea that wanting to be happy *simply is* taking the attitude "Every man for himself." This is a great secret: if I am only for myself, then I am not for myself. For human beings the good life is not good until we have others with whom to share it. One can imagine rational beings whose happiness has nothing to do with the happiness of others, but if there are any such beings, we are not they. Besides, if I know nothing about how to be happy, then how can I know anything about helping others to be happy? Happiness involves a *partnership* in a good life, and I am as much a member of the partnership as my partners in it are.

I hear the third objection mostly from people who have studied the philosopher Immanuel Kant. They say that if we pursue happiness then we are not free—because to make some good our goal is to allow our wills to be "determined" by some consideration external to them. This time what is right about the objection is that our wills are, and ought to be, free. But what do the objectors suppose the will, and its freedom, to be?

Think of it like this: There are two kinds of appetite, or desire. One is sensual appetite, which pulls us toward whatever seems good to the senses. The other is rational appetite, which urges us toward whatever seems good to the judgment of the mind. Now our will *simply is* our rational appetite. This is why our wills cannot be severed from our judgments of the good—for even if our judgments are mistaken, it is impossible to will anything whatsoever except for the reason that it seems good to us and worthy of pursuit. And so the freedom of the will is not a freedom *not to be determined* by judgments of the good, but a freedom *to make* such judgments. It is the liberty of the rational being to deliberate, to recognize what matters, and to decide what is really good—another of his differences from "every other creature in the natural world." So of course it is not slavery to seek happiness. The pursuit of fulfillment for ourselves and for others is freedom's proper use.

The fourth objection is that because there are some things we shouldn't do for any reason whatsoever, we shouldn't pursue happiness, but duty. What is right about this objection is that there really are such things as intrinsically evil deeds—such as murder or failing in certain duties—deeds that cannot be justified by anything at all. But what is an intrinsically evil deed? It is not a deed that we must not commit even for the sake of the good; it is a deed that *by its very nature cannot* be directed to the good. The conclusion to be drawn from the existence of intrinsically evil deeds is not that we should pursue duty instead of fulfillment, but that failure in our duties is not fulfillment. Those who think that intrinsically evil deeds can make us happy are usually confusing happiness with some sort of emotional satisfaction. A cruel man delights in his cruelty, true. But this kind of delight is not happiness. I willingly concede that there is a lot packed into that claim. For now, I just want to put it on the table.

The final objection—not the last one anyone could think of (there is never an end to those), but the last to be considered here—is that our greatest good isn't being happy, but knowing God. What this objection gets right is that there is nothing more important than knowing God. Where it goes wrong is to assume that finding God and attaining supreme happiness are two different things, as though one could have either supreme happiness without God, or God without supreme happiness. But what if in some sense, God *simply is* our supreme happiness?

Hold on! A moment ago I was on the verge of losing readers who believe in God—and now I am on the verge of losing those who don't!

God-phobes, take heart. You can turn off the alarms. Although this book takes questions about the relationship of happiness to God seriously, those questions don't come up again until much, much later in the book, and all (or almost all) of what I say up to that point should make sense equally to those who believe in Him and those who don't.

So if you wish, you can read up to that point and then stop.

But I hope you don't.

I do understand the fear of going off the edge. You may believe not just that you don't know about God but that knowledge about God is rationally unattainable. If this were true, then the moment we began thinking about Him we would have to cast reason to the winds. Not many people want to be irrational. Nor should they. Concerning this fear, I don't ask for final trust; I do ask for provisional trust. Reserve judgment about whether I am leading you off the edge until later in the book.

I have given fair warning of what comes later. But it comes much later. For now, we will lay these matters aside. No God for many chapters—I promise. Our topic is simply how and how not to be happy.

# CHAPTER 2

## How Not to Find the Answer to the Question— and How to Find It

"If, then, there is some end of the things we do, which we
desire for its own sake...if we do not choose everything for
the sake of something else...clearly this must be the good
and the chief good. Will not the knowledge of it, then, have a
great influence on life?"[1]

The nineteenth-century economist F. Y. Edgeworth believed that some day we would have instruments to measure happiness, just as we have instruments to measure temperature.[2] Imagine a physician's assistant putting a happiness thermometer in your ear and reporting the result: "Mr. Jones, the readout shows that you are experiencing only 5.6 units of bliss. Are you feeling a bit off today?"

The notion is absurd. True, some day we may be able to measure whether someone is feeling good, perhaps by monitoring the electrical activity in the pleasure center of the brain. But to call a measurement of feelings a measurement of happiness is to beg the important question of how happiness and feelings are related. To paraphrase the philosopher Mortimer Adler, it is one thing to ask whether a person is having a good time, and another to ask whether he is having a good life.[3] The latter is more like what we mean by happiness, and it isn't a matter of his momentary feelings.

So we can't measure happiness with instruments—unless by this we mean the instrument of thoughtful conversation. The only way to know what makes people happy is to talk with them.

To talk with them? Does that mean just asking a lot of people "What makes you happy?" and collating all of the answers?

No, but a great many psychologists seem to think that it does. One reason they think so is the relativistic notion that each person's "construct" of happiness is equally valid. From this point of view, you must know whether you are happy, because *by definition*, happiness for you is whatever you say it is. One fellow says, "My happiness is making money." Another says, "My happiness is having pleasure." Yet another says, "My happiness is being a social butterfly." Each to his own!

As usual, there is something in the idea—but that doesn't make it wholly, or even mostly, true. In this case, what's true in the idea is the fact that individual differences count for something. If you are cut out for raising a family, you may be unhappy as a bachelor. If you are clumsy with your hands, you may be unhappy as a carpenter. If you have just a few close friends, you may be unhappy having associations with a lot of people forced upon you. But there are general laws of happiness too, because some things *universally* militate for and against human fulfillment. Since we share the same human nature, it is hard to see how this could be false.

Other psychologists grasp that there may be universal laws of happiness, but they still think that to find out what they are, all we have to do is collate the answers to the question, "What makes you happy?" They assume that even if happiness isn't *by definition* what each person says it is, still each person knows whether he is happy and what makes him that way. But is that true?

This time what is right in the idea is that most people know *something* about happiness. Since we human beings have inside knowledge of our own minds, it would be impossible for us not to know something about it. If we didn't, we wouldn't even know that there is such a thing. Indeed, since outside of the most mindless fantasies there are no such things as happiness thermometers, if people didn't already know something about happiness, we could never find out more about it. For where else but there could we start?

But consider: Even if happiness *were* just having good feelings, do people always know how they are feeling? All day Tuesday, Mr. Jones snaps at everyone around him. His wife knows that he is feeling grouchy. His children know. His co-workers know. Yet he may be oblivious to the fact. All day Wednesday, Mrs. Jones is withdrawn. "Is something the matter, dear?" her husband asks. "Nothing's the matter! Why don't you leave me alone?" One of the reasons we have difficulty controlling our moods is that we don't always know that we are in them.

And knowing whether we are happy is a good deal harder than knowing how we feel. Though we tend to overlook the fact, it is possible to have a share in happiness without knowing it. A young husband and wife may be so absorbed in caring for their family that it never occurs to them that they are happy. Yet many years later, looking back over their memories, they smile and say, "We were happy, weren't we?" For that matter, although someone who says he is miserable is no doubt correct, it is possible to be *unhappy* without knowing it. If I have never had much experience of true happiness, I may not have much idea of what it would be like. Perhaps things "seem to be going all right" and I am surrounded by the accoutrements of what my friends all call success, so when asked "Are you happy?" I answer, "Yeah, I guess so." Yet I may not be happy at all.

Consider, too, that although one can judge feelings at a moment in time, judging happiness at a moment in time is a different kettle of fish. Suppose you are halfway through a novel. If I ask you whether it is a good novel, you may answer, "I don't know yet—ask me when I've finished it!" You may be able to tell me whether you've been enjoying it, but whether it is a good novel is not the same thing as whether it has kept you in a continuous state of enjoyment. There may be things on every page to titillate your attention, yet the story may not hang together as a whole. The happiness of a life is like that. It isn't just a series of enjoyments, and its happiness may be difficult to gauge until it is done. The goodness of a life is a lot like the goodness of a true story.

So far in this chapter I have maintained two propositions: First, that the chief way to know what makes people happy is to talk with them, and second, that this *doesn't* mean just asking them what makes them happy. What I am leading up to is that since we do have inside knowledge about our minds, it makes very good sense to begin with common opinions about happiness, but it doesn't make good sense to end with them.

Objections could be raised to either of the claims of that last sentence: that it makes sense to begin with common opinions, or that it doesn't make good sense to end with them. Let's think about this.

As to the first claim in that sentence above, someone might suggest that to begin with common opinion is merely to follow the mob. Isn't this the *ad populum* fallacy, the appeal to the crowd? There is such a fallacy, but this isn't it. I am asking people about something within their own subjective experience—inside knowledge, as I have called it—not about, say, the microbial causes of tuberculosis or the frequency of cometary collisions with Jupiter. What the crowd thinks about those causes or about the frequency of those collisions has no value. What they think about their own experience does.

Consider my experience of my relationship with my friend. From the outside, it may seem much the same as my relationship with my grocer, because in both cases both parties expect to receive equal good from each other. Yet the two cases are not really the same, because one is a relationship of justice, but the other is a relationship of love. Both the grocer and I are keeping score. I want to be sure that he gave me all the groceries I paid for; he wants to be sure that I gave him the full price of my groceries. By contrast, friends delight in small sacrifices for each other and disdain to keep score. If my friend pays for a soft drink from the dispenser because I am out of change, he will be insulted if I say a week later, "Here's the change that I owe you." Now how would I know this if I had never had a friend? Or how could I explain to someone who had never had a friend? This is inside knowledge.

Or consider love. A new father remarked to me that there are certain things about a father's love that seem obvious now, but of which he hadn't the slightest inkling before his child was born. He told me that if anyone had tried to explain these things to him, he wouldn't have understood. Yet now that he was actually caring for his child, those things were as plain to him as his nose. This is another instance of inside knowledge. Husbands and wives know that there are certain things about each other that they couldn't have known except by submitting to the sweet discipline of mutual love and trust. Thomas Aquinas calls such knowledge connatural, meaning that when I love someone, my nature adapts itself to that person; the other person's nature becomes second nature to me.[4] These things, too, are inside knowledge.

Moreover, I am not inquiring into passing fancies but into considered views that have endured across societies and centuries—the inside knowledge of many generations. Not that I don't *mention* the fashionable opinions of the moment. Often, I do. But I don't use them as oracles of truth. Rather I use them because they illustrate, exaggerate, or contradict considered views that have been around for a long, long time. By the way, I also take into account the opinions of the wise—or more precisely, of those who are commonly accounted wise—because the opinions of those whose reputation for wisdom has endured over many generations is a proper extension of opinions common over many generations.

Still disputing the first claim of that sentence that I set down a few paragraphs ago—my assertion that it makes very good sense to *begin* with common opinions about happiness—someone might suggest that we have other data too. What about direct observation? If someone weeps all the time, has screaming fits, or commits suicide, surely it is reasonable to conclude that he is not happy? I would reply, "Yes and no." Such things are certainly evidence of unhappiness. But how do we know that they are? Only by falling back on common opinion, on what everyone knows. *We all understand* that happy persons may whistle, make birdhouses, and enjoy conversations, and that they don't constantly weep, scream, and commit suicide.

Now as to the second claim of that sentence, about not *ending* with common opinion (as extended by the opinions of those commonly accounted wise): If common opinion about happiness is our only ordinary source of data,[5] then how can we get beyond it?

We get beyond it by making it cross-examine itself.

I mentioned in the preface that even ideas that are mostly mistaken must have some grain of truth in them, otherwise no one could believe them. The task is to sift through our ideas in order to separate the grain from the chaff. The way to do this is not to pull ideas out of the blue, but to "assemble reminders" of things we think we know and use them to reconsider other things we think we know. Wise persons are those who have done this well. Wise doctrines embody the results of this procedure. Reflecting upon them, we say, "How could I not have seen that? I see it now!" True, sometimes we may accept what a wise teacher says about something on faith, even if we do not yet see it for ourselves—but in general, we will not trust his wisdom unless he has gained our confidence by all the other things he has already helped us to see.

My favorite example of making common opinion cross-examine itself comes from one of the Socratic dialogues, the *Gorgias*. One of the persons in the dialogue, a crass fellow named Callicles, invokes the common opinion that happiness lies in continually having the greatest possible appetites and continually having the power to satisfy them. Socrates backs him into a corner by asking whether in this case, it would be desirable to itch as much as possible, but always be able to scratch. Ashamed to contradict himself, Callicles says yes. In his characteristically brilliant but annoying way, Socrates goes on to make Callicles commit himself to more and more ridiculous and even disgusting positions. For example, by asking whether the itching must extend to every part of the body, he forces Callicles to concede that even a catamite—a boy or man who seeks to be sexually penetrated—would have to be considered happy so long as he kept getting what he wanted. Callicles won't admit that he is wrong, but it is clear to those who are listening that he has lost the round.

Now what has happened here? There are several grains of truth in the way Callicles appeals to common opinion. He is not mistaken—and people in general are not mistaken—to think that happiness has something to do with the satisfaction of desire. He is not mistaken—and people in general are not mistaken—to think that anything rightly deserving the name "happiness" would be abiding rather than fleeting, something not easy to lose. The problem is that Callicles does not separate the grain from the chaff. He lumps all desires together, good and bad; he thinks that to moderate any desire is to be as good as dead; and he does not consider the *sense* in which true happiness would have to abide. Is it merely like the fullness of a bathtub with the faucet pouring in at the top, but the drain wide open at the bottom?

One might think that to show Callicles's error Socrates would have to go *outside* of common opinion. On the contrary, he appeals to common opinion himself. For if Callicles were right, there would be nothing happier than the most intense and continuous itching and the most intense and continuous scratching—*and can't we all see that this is false?*

Through this little exchange, has Socrates shown what happiness *is?* Not at all, nor does he claim to have shown us. Winning through to the truth of the matter takes much more time and requires better conversational partners than Callicles.

But even the accumulation of exploded errors is progress. Little by little, we get there. Eventually we may be able to figure out the decisive questions—to ask them, and perhaps even to answer them.

# CHAPTER 3

# *What We All Mean by Happiness—Whatever It Is*

"I don't want just words. If that's all you have for me,
you'd better go."[1]

Costello: Well then who's on first?
Abbott: Yes!
Costello: I mean the fellow's name!
Abbott: Who!
Costello: The guy on first!
Abbott: Who!
Costello: The first baseman!
Abbott: Who!
Costello: The guy playing first!
Abbott: Who is on first!
Costello: Now whaddya askin' me for?
Abbott: I'm telling you Who is on first.
Costello: Well, I'm asking YOU who's on first!
Abbott: That's the man's name.
Costello: That's who's name?
Abbott: Yes.
Costello: Well go ahead and tell me.
Abbott: Who.[2]

One of the difficulties of inquiring into how and how not to be happy is that people use the term "happiness" in different ways and so end up talking past each other. For example, suppose we ask whether happiness is the same as pleasure, but one of the persons in the conversation uses the word "happiness" simply to *mean* pleasure. If that's how he uses the word, he won't understand the question at all. It will seem to him like asking whether all bachelors are unmarried. Of course they are; that is what it means to be a bachelor. The kind of question we are *trying* to ask, however, is more like whether all bachelors have brown hair.

It isn't as hard to talk about happiness as all that. Sometimes, even though different things called by the same name lack a single common element, we find that each of the meanings of the term depends in some way on a single clear case. For example, a "healthy" diet, a "healthy" medicine, a "healthy" complexion, and a "healthy" man have no common element, yet the first is related to health in the sense that it preserves health, the second in the sense that it produces health, the third in the sense that it is a symptom of health, and the fourth in the sense that it has health.[3]

In the same way, the "happiness" of a diner who is satisfied with his meal may have no element in common with the "happiness" of a child on a merry-go-round, and neither of them may have any element in common with the "happiness" of Henry V's soldiers:

> This story shall the good man teach his son;
> And Crispin Crispian shall ne'er go by,
> From this day to the ending of the world,
> But we in it shall be rememberèd—
> We few, we happy few, we band of brothers;
> For he to-day that sheds his blood with me
> Shall be my brother; be he ne'er so vile,

> This day shall gentle his condition;
> And gentlemen in England now a-bed
> Shall think themselves accurs'd they were not here,
> And hold their manhoods cheap whiles any speaks
> That fought with us upon Saint Crispin's day.[4]

Presumably we use the term happiness for all these different things because we suppose that *supreme and unqualified* happiness would have something to do with all these different things— something to do with enjoyment, but also something to do with nobility and glory.

So let us be clear: We are asking in this book whether *supreme* happiness can be had, and if so how. But before asking about its attainment we must be as clear as possible about what we mean by it.

The shortest characterization of happiness is Aristotle's: happiness is living well and doing well.[5] When I was a young man, this definition annoyed me because it didn't tell me in what living well and doing well consists. But that is not the point of a definition; explanations of that sort come afterward. Even so, we can give a much more complete characterization of supreme and unqualified happiness than Aristotle's "living well and doing well." From everyday conversation and classical literature, I think we can say the following things too.

To be happy in the unqualified sense is the same as to be fulfilled, to flourish, or to thrive—to enjoy complete well-being, to have our complete and final good. Nothing that fails to fulfill us, no condition inimical to our flourishing, no state in which we cannot thrive is rightly called happiness. If someone says, "I am languishing and thoroughly unfulfilled, yet completely happy," we would not say, "Apparently happiness is not fulfillment." We would say he was confused about the meaning of the word "happiness," and perhaps addled in his wits.

But if this is how we use the term, then it follows that unqualified happiness cannot coexist with its opposite. It is no more possible to be completely happy and unhappy at the same time than to be thriving and perishing at the same time. True, someone can be more or less happy, but we are not speaking of being more or less. Not that we will scorn what we can learn of partial happiness, but learning the merely partial is not our final goal.

Furthermore, we understand happiness in the unqualified sense to be something abiding rather than fleeting. Nothing that is here today and gone tomorrow deserves to be called supreme happiness; we use the term more for a property of a life than of a moment. Whether there can be such a thing is a separate question. For now it is enough to say that if I was happy on Tuesday but not on Wednesday, then the "happiness" I enjoyed on Tuesday was not the sort of happiness we are asking about.

One of the consequences of the fact that happiness is abiding is that happiness is independent of the caprices of others. Granted, we need other people, and we care for their regard. But if we are slaves to them—if they can bestow or destroy our happiness at a whim—then whatever we get from them is not happiness.

Unqualified happiness is not only something we long for, but something we can't help but long for. The longing seems rooted in our nature; it is our deepest and most persistent desire. We would not use the term "happiness" for anything to which we could be indifferent.

We seek other things for the sake of such happiness, yet we seek happiness itself for its own sake. Someone who seeks wealth for the sake of fulfillment may be on either the right track or the wrong one, like someone who puts sugar in the cookies for the sake of making them sweet. But it would make no more sense to say, "I seek fulfillment for the sake of wealth" than to say "I try to make the cookies sweet so that they will have sugar in them." Such statements would be inane.

By supreme and unqualified happiness, we also mean something *sufficient,* something complete and lacking nothing. If someone lacked some necessity, we might be willing to call him happy in a qualified, an imperfect, or an incomplete sense, but we would not call him supremely happy.

Just because we do think of supreme happiness as lacking nothing, we think of it as something that would satisfy our deepest longings so fully that nothing would be left to be desired. Now it may turn out to be the case that in order to attain this state, our desires would have to change—some thinkers have thought so. We will have to look into that. For now it suffices to say that we are not begging any questions; there is a big difference between saying that happiness would leave nothing to be desired and saying that having everything that we presently desire would make us happy.

Finally, since one of our deep longings is to be good and noble rather than wicked and base, happiness must be compatible with the splendor of virtue and incompatible with its lack. Whether to be happy it is *enough* to be good and noble, as supposed in the St. Crispin's day speech, is another question, which we will have to investigate later. Even so, we do not call vicious persons happy, even if they are pleased with themselves.

This then is the focal meaning of happiness. Every human language has a word for it, because every human mind has at least a dim idea of it. Whether the thing that the word names can be attained at all, and if so, how and to what degree, is a matter of great interest to human beings in every age, and the preoccupation of this book.

Since now you know how I am using the term, we can reason together and perhaps find out the answers to these questions. Someone may, of course, say, "But what you have just described is not how

*I* speak of unqualified or supreme happiness." Perhaps, but it seems to me that it is how almost everyone does. I will continue to appeal to the common sense of the matter as we continue—as I said before, not ending with common opinion, but beginning with it.

One can imagine a radically different method. Someone might suggest, "Suppose we take happiness to mean Q," whereby Q is something of interest to him, but disconnected from shared human experience. In that case I think his answers would be of no interest to other human beings either.

Or he might accept the method I have been following but say that I have followed it badly. Well, if he can follow it better, more power to him! I could easily be mistaken, and if I am, I hope to be shown how I am wrong. So far, though, I don't see how I could be. If he said, for example, "We *don't* desire something abiding. All that we desire are momentary attractions, aversions, and responses," I would say he is mistaken. Though some fleeting experiences are precious to us, introspection shows that we also desire something more than what fleets.

A really radical critic might even say that introspection is nonsense. For example, he may say that our sense that we have such things as reasons, purposes, and will is an illusion—of an order with thinking that rivers are inhabited by spirits that make them flow downhill. He thinks these supposed mental experiences are not real but mythical, not real explanations of our behavior but rationalizations cooked up afterward to explain it to ourselves.

This sort of objection can be answered in several ways. In the first place, if the critic were right, he would never know it, because his own theory would be a rationalization too. There would be no reason for him to consider his own theoretical constructs any less mythical than the commonsense view that we do have reasons, purposes, and will. After all, in devising his own theory, does he suppose that he is doing something *other than* reasoning about the truth of the matter and exercising his will?

In the second place, if reason and will are illusions, then why do we have such illusions? Why do we *need* to explain our behavior to ourselves? Why don't we just behave as we are going to behave, spontaneously, unconsciously, without explanation, like hydras that flinch when they are touched, or insects that fly toward the light? It seems that the need to come up with illusory rationalizations for our behavior would be a pointless diversion of energy from the great work of—well, of whatever our nervous system is making us do. The dog doesn't need a theory of motivation to eat his dog food; he just eats it. We would be the same. *But we aren't.* Presumably the value of the commonsense idea that we have such things as reason and will lies in the fact that we have them.

Of course I have no illusion that I can answer all objections, for humans love objections and are endlessly inventive in devising them. It seems to be possible for us to quarrel about anything whatsoever. The philosopher Descartes thought that we should refuse to accept any starting point of thought that can be doubted—but this is absurd, because everything can be doubted.

Descartes famously thought that *not* everything could be doubted. That is the point of his famous *cogito ergo sum*: I cannot doubt my own existence, because here I am thinking about it. But he was quite mistaken, for I can doubt even whether I am thinking. Someone might reply on his behalf, "But if there is a thought, then doesn't there have to be someone to think it?" Even supposing this to be true, why must the someone be me? Perhaps someone else is thinking "my" thoughts; I might even be a simulation on someone's mainframe. Besides, who says that thoughts require thinkers at all? We may suppose that thinkers produce thoughts, but how do we know that free-floating thoughts don't produce the illusion of minds thinking them? Or that minds are merely part of what these thoughts are thoughts of?

Mind you, I am not proposing such a method. I think the method of doubting everything that can be doubted is madness. Rather we should believe what we have the best reasons to believe—until we are given better reasons to believe something different.

But in order to keep from being bogged down by endless objections, something else is necessary, too. We must agree on the purpose of our conversation: we must cooperate in searching for the truth, rather than quarreling with no regard for it merely to win the argument.

Some people think that any effort to show that a given view is mistaken is arguing just to win the argument. I disagree. But there is something to be said for their view. For if the conversation is to be really cooperative, then whenever possible, one must try to give full credit to what is true even in mistaken views, to give full weight to the element in the mistaken view that makes it plausible, even if it is ultimately wrong.

For example, suppose someone claims that all dogs have four legs. All we need to do to refute this view is point to a three-legged dog. But suppose the other fellow responded, "But I don't think that's a dog." He is wrong—but doesn't he have a point? Rather than just pointing to the three-legged dog, it might be more helpful to make a distinction: *By nature,* dogs do have four legs. *Accidentally,* through some defect, a particular dog may have only three.

Now the other side may not be won over. But I think this procedure gives a better chance of showing why the other side ought to be won over, even if it isn't. If I should be found to deviate from this procedure at times—though I will try not to—I hope at least that I will adhere to it closely enough to inspire some readers to do better.

# PART TWO

## Getting On with It

"I begin to perceive a track, and I believe that the quarry
will not escape."[1]

# CHAPTER 4

# Could Wealth Be Happiness?

"Annual income twenty pounds, annual expenditure nineteen
nineteen and six, result happiness. Annual income twenty
pounds, annual expenditure twenty pounds ought and six,
result misery."[1]

T here are two common opinions about wealth: That having a
lot of it is happiness, and that it isn't. People on both sides
think the matter is obvious.

The former view is expressed by the author of a self-help book
who advises, "learn how rich people think, copy them, take action
and get rich." He offers his readers a series of pithy adages, including
"middle class believes hard work creates wealth, world class believes
leverage creates wealth," "middle class believes money is the root of
all evil, world class believes poverty is the root of all evil," and "middle class worries about money, world class dreams about money."
Besides the original edition, his book comes in both a condensed
edition and a "Simple Truths Gift Box," each of which advertises that
it can be read in an hour—presumably for people who want to get
rich very, very quickly.[2]

Persons who make wealth their chief pursuit don't necessarily
think that money, material wealth, and possessions are the only

things that matter. Rather they believe that those are the things that matter *most* and the means of obtaining all the other things that matter too. It is as though the biblical saying had been inverted to read, "Seek first the kingdom of opulence, and all these things shall be added to you."[3]

Something in our inherited wisdom calls this view odious. Yet such books sell well; quite a few readers must find their conviction persuasive. Can a case be made for it?

It may seem not. As one very old theory has it, only a few demented misers want wealth for its own sake. Almost everyone seeks it for the sake of something else. Therefore, even in the view of the wealth-lovers themselves, happiness cannot be wealth; it must be something else. There is some force to this argument, but in the end, isn't it a little glib? It succeeds in showing that wealth isn't happiness *in itself.* On the other hand, it fails to refute the more common view that wealth is the *means* to being happy, the highway for getting there.

Many of us were taught when we were small that "money can't buy happiness." I found the saying confusing. Children like pieties, and repeating this one gave me a pleasantly pious feeling—but was it true? It was certainly true in one way: I knew my parents couldn't go to the store and purchase a package labeled "happiness." But couldn't they buy things that would *make* them happy? Challenged, my mother—a wise woman—replied that, although money can purchase many things, it can't purchase things like friendship, which happiness requires. Yes, I saw that—although I had once bribed another child with a stick of chewing gum to play with me instead of with the other kid. But doesn't money purchase lots of other things that are also important to happiness? I couldn't imagine not having food, shelter, and clothing. And I could hardly imagine doing without my toys.

We grown-ups feel much the same about our grown-up toys. I once attended a conference at which a lot of things were said against hedonism and materialism. The discussion was just a little bit smug. Finally one scholar in the audience lost patience and burst out: "What's wrong with Cuisinarts?"

My wife, a consummate cook and master seamstress, would say that my anecdote is unjust to Cuisinart. Her food processor is not a *toy*. Like her serger and sewing machine, it is an instrument of the domestic arts, a tool for the furtherance of certain distinctively human powers in the context of family life. Not only does the exercise of these arts contribute to our home, but they are intrinsically rewarding to her. She loves and takes pride in them. Just watching her use her talents is a pleasure; I always think of the glowing beauty of Vermeer's painting *The Lacemaker*. Her imagination, thoughtfulness, selflessness, taste, and sense of beauty in their pursuit are what the philosopher Alasdair MacIntyre would call "virtues internal to the practice" of domesticity.[4]

Now my wife's cooking and sewing tools are certainly material things, and by using them she also *makes* material things, like meals and clothing. But her use of them for the practice of her arts isn't any more "materialistic" than my use of a computer to write this book, or a carpenter's use of his hammer, level, ruler, nails, and saw to build a house. One of the rewards of the crafts is the practice of the crafts themselves, and their practice is not a material possession. Yet the tools of the crafts must be purchased with money—and they are forms of material wealth, aren't they?

It seems, then, that even for things that are not wealth—such as the crafts—we need a certain quantum of wealth. Since we are not disembodied souls, but souls united with bodies, it could hardly be otherwise. We must employ material instrumentalities, which are forms of wealth, to live in the world at all: not only for acquiring food, clothing, and shelter, but even for the practice of powers without which we would hardly feel human.

Let me add one more thing in favor of wealth: It is cruel to tell a starving man, "Be content with what you have." I hope this doesn't need to be explained.

Now any view of the relation between happiness and wealth that ignored such facts would be nonsense. Yet if we are honest, we also find that many other things about wealth and its possession suggest that it can be an impediment to happiness.

First, there is a great difference between the idea that we need certain material goods for living and the idea that the more we have the better we live. I am trying to avoid statistics, but this is one of the times I will indulge. Let us assume that whatever happiness is, people who commit suicide are not happy. Interestingly, the suicide rate among Americans has increased 35 percent since the turn of the millennium.[5] Now if wealth leads to happiness, one might expect suicide rates to plunge among the rich, but what the data actually show us is more complicated. For example, a study in 2012 showed that although persons earning less than $10,000 a year have a 50 percent greater suicide risk than persons with incomes over $60,000, further increases in income don't make much difference to suicide rates. Moreover, wealthy people tend to live among other wealthy people, and interestingly, suicide rates *rise* when people live in wealthy neighborhoods.[6] Researchers speculate that the problem isn't so much that the wealthy don't have enough wealth as that they can't all have as much as their rich neighbors. They think they have to keep up with the Joneses. And this state of mind seems to plague the rich more than the moderately poor, for otherwise the wealth of the neighborhood would make no difference; the anxiety of comparison would drive everyone *equally* to suicide. As one writer observes, "Competitive, insecure, status-obsessed communities operate like lifelong middle schools"[7]—a chilling thought indeed.

Everyday observation suggests that having too much wealth is especially harmful to the young. An older person who has come up the hard way may be able to handle his wealth because in the course of attaining it he developed personal qualities such as diligence, prudence, personal responsibility, and restraint. His child, who has had every material thing he desired almost before the desire could be formulated, may find even the easy life of a rich man difficult to live because these virtues are alien to him; he has had no chance to attain them. And what is he living for anyway? Is a human being merely a "consumer"? It is better to have the chance to earn something than simply to own it.

It also seems to be the case that people don't always know what they want. Thinking, "I have to get rich," someone may develop skill in starting and managing businesses. Yet after his empire is established and he has all the money that he thought he wanted, he may grow bored. Desiring a new challenge, he sells the old business and starts all over again with a new one. Could it be that he was more interested in the making of money than in the money itself? In fact, could it be that it wasn't the making of it that he enjoyed either, but the exercise of the practical arts of business? Perhaps sheer wealth never really was what pleased him most; rather he viewed it as a sign that he was doing well in his real purpose, the exercise of the activity of business. This shouldn't be surprising, for we have already seen, in connection with keeping up with the Joneses, that wealth can be a stand-in for other things. Perhaps someone craves the admiration of others; the larger his house and the more expensive his car, the more he thinks others admire him.

Possessions "get old." Someone buys a shiny new possession, and at first it thrills him, but the thrill wears off. In fact, it can wear off pretty quickly. "When we desire or solicit anything," wrote Jonathan Swift, "our minds run wholly on the good side or circumstances of it; when it is obtained, our minds run wholly on the bad ones."[8] And there is this problem too: the disappointment of losing something is often greater than the enjoyment of having it. Joseph Addison suggested that this happens because "in the enjoyment of an object we only find that share of pleasure which it is capable of giving us, but in the loss of it we do not proportion our grief to the real value it bears, but to the value our fancies and imaginations set upon it."[9] Thus, a person bored with his possession may eventually reach the point at which he gets very little enjoyment from having it, yet he would be angry and upset if he could no longer have it.[10]

Yet another insight about the pains of needless possession crops up over and over in classical literature. Lady Philosophy warns Boethius that because riches are fleeting, the rich man has many cares and may be consumed by his anxieties. Wealth, she says, gleams more splendidly when given than when kept; the best thing about having it is being able to give it away. By doing so, the giver relieves not only the need of the receiver but also his own burden of possession. This dual good is why generosity has traditionally been viewed as a virtue and stinginess as a vice.[11]

Do we understand these things about ourselves? Yes and no; we know them, but we forget them. If I am asked, "Does this possession make you happy?" I may think of how pleased I was when I acquired it, but I probably fail to consider how pleased with it I am now. Or I may think of how much I enjoy having it but fail to consider my anxiety lest something happens to it. I may even think that this anxiety shows *how much* it means to me, even though, as we have just seen, that is really a different question.

We imagine that wealth will shield us from suffering, but that is a crock of lies. Not only does everyone suffer, but very little good comes without some suffering, and our appreciation of the goods we do possess is deepened by it. Speaking for myself, I learned almost nothing during the easy periods of my life; every insight, every blessing was hard-won. I learned what a fool I can be through disaster, and how much I really loved my father when he was failing and depended on me. I learned what a treasure my wife is when we struggled together through hardship, and the blessing of fatherhood through all of that lost sleep and sacrifice. We tend to detest suffering while we are actually enduring it, but long afterward we may be profoundly grateful for it. I would never have chosen to be unemployed, and I would never wish unemployment on anyone else, yet I am grateful to have had the experience. Even looking forward, suffering appears different to me from how it did when I was young. John Donne was right: in some respects, "affliction is a treasure, and scarce any man hath enough of it."[12]

Irrespective of our religious backgrounds, most of us have heard the beatitude, "Blessed are the poor." Since I have promised not to talk about God until much later in the book, I will not now inquire into the spiritual significance of the saying. But it makes some sense even from a this-worldly perspective. Blessedness means supreme happiness. Although there is nothing blessed about being so utterly destitute that I cannot even feed my hungry children, there is a certain blessing that is denied to the rich and belongs only to the everyday poor, to those who live in what Dorothy Day called "decent poverty."[13] Whatever their grave disadvantages—which are many—at least they are spared the delusion of thinking that humans can place ultimate reliance in their wealth. For that is the god in which the rich are tempted to place final trust, and whether or not there is a true God, *that* god is certainly false; it cannot bear the weight of adoration.

Yet behind the false promise of wealth is something inescapably true, for however confused we may be, the idea of happiness does include the idea of sufficiency. The question is: Sufficiency of what? What do we really need to have enough of? Although the reflections in this chapter should warn us against placing ultimate trust in wealth, we do not have to succumb to the opposite fallacy of "angelism," viewing ourselves as though we were immaterial beings who had no material needs. Danger lies both in not having enough of what we need and in having too much. Rather than gaining as much wealth as possible, we should learn to be satisfied with enough to live according to our station in life, or a little below it, comparing ourselves with our neighbors as little as possible. The wealthiest people tend to have the hardest time doing this.

Granted, since humans are social beings, it may be impossible not to compare ourselves with others *at all*. If my shoes have holes, I will be ashamed, even if I am indoors and it makes no difference to the comfort of my feet. Still, we can try to compare ourselves *less than we do*. That is difficult, but aren't all of the virtues difficult? So is patience. So is courage. So is honesty.

# CHAPTER 5

# Could Bodily Health or Beauty Be Happiness?

"Beauty vanishes like a vapor—
Preach the men of musty morals."[1]

O ne might think that the notion that health is happiness, or that beauty is happiness, is found only in schlocky advertisements and inspirational books. Far from it. The idea is even promoted at one of the websites of the United Nations Development Program, praising the attitude it attributes to the inhabitants of Bhutan: "Health is Happiness." Note the prestigious agency's radicalism. Not content to say that health is helpful to happiness, that it is necessary for happiness, or even that it is a constituent of happiness, it claims that the two things are identical.

But carelessly dismissing the idea would also radically underestimate its grip on us. In the previous chapter we were talking about wealth; let's think for a moment about how much wealth we lavish on our bodies.

Expenditures for health care take up almost a fifth of the economy.[2] If we add in health and fitness clubs and gyms, the proportion is greater still. The weight loss and diet industry shows modest growth even though fewer Americans are dieting. And the reason that fewer are dieting seems to be not so much that they are less concerned with their bodies, but that they are less concerned with the *weight* of their bodies—a very different thing, since one of the current fads is that fat can be beautiful too.[3] (The painter Titian would agree.) The market for cosmetics and beauty products, including both skin and hair care, grows significantly faster than the rest of the economy. Economists and market researchers are so impressed by the resilience of this sector during recessions that they have given it a name: the "lipstick effect." This term is somewhat misleading, though, because the market for men's cosmetics and fragrances—sometimes called the "metrosexual" market—is also soaring.[4]

Of course, some of the money spent on clothing is about need rather than looks; our bodies require protection from the elements. But they don't require *stylish* protection from the elements, and high-end fashion and lingerie, which are more about beauty than need, do very well. So do fragrances.

Let's think about health first. One reason we take an interest in it is to be able to get on with our lives, to do things that matter to us. If I am chronically ill, then I will find it difficult to hold a job, take care of my children, and accomplish my purposes in life. Now one would think that this factor in the interest in health would be a historical constant, for don't all people in all times want to get on with their lives? But if so, then how do we explain the *increase* in interest in health?

One part of the explanation seems to be that people today are more afraid of death than people in the past. In an era in which life is short and grim, people view death as inevitable. In an era like ours, when average lifespan is increasing, even though death is just as inevitable one might imagine that it can be put off indefinitely. Not only that, but fewer people subscribe to supernatural religions today than in times past, and the belief that when we die we are nothing but worm food produces in many people a determination to keep living to the last second possible.

Now it may seem that the fear of bodily sickness, affliction, and imperfection would be another historical constant, like wanting to get on with our lives. No one wants to be ill. But this fear is not a constant either; the same causes that impel the people of our day to a greater fear of death also impel us to a greater fear of sickness. The image of life going out like a snuffed candle obsesses us with the thought of our fragility and drives us to remain in control; like death itself, illness imperils that control.

These feelings are not simple. Paradoxically, for the sake of the illusion of control, some people even bring death on themselves, as though to say, *I am the master! I decide! If I cannot cheat death, then I will cheat life itself!* Others are so obsessed with bodily infirmity that they find embodiment itself an encumbrance. In contrast with the Psalmist, who famously reflects that he is "fearfully and wonderfully made,"[5] an online writer remarks, "The fact that I'm a squishy bag of water freaks me out constantly: Thinking about how fragile and necessarily *ad hoc* my respiratory and circulatory systems are, contemplating the various fluids and other things my body excretes, and of course, sex. Corporeal existence is weird and sometimes very inconvenient."[6]

More commonly, though, we cringe in horror not from the mere thought of having bodies but from pain, sickness, weakness, incapacity, and the decay of the appearance of youth. A writer recovering from alcoholism describes his awakening from a night filled with hallucinations of spiders. "If I died, it would be okay," he says, adding that "the cliché *When you have your health, you have everything* is very true. When you do not have your health, nothing else matters at all."[7] He might almost have been channeling the morose thinker

Arthur Schopenhauer, who wrote, "With health everything is a source of pleasure; without it, nothing else, whatever it may be, is enjoyable.... It follows from all this that the greatest of follies is to sacrifice health for any other kind of happiness, whatever it may be."[8]

One would have to be a heel not to sympathize with suffering, but sympathy does not justify fallacy. Even if it were true that to lack health were to lack everything else, it does not follow that to have health is to have everything else, for a lot of healthy people are unhappy. And the premise isn't true anyway. Although lack of health is an obstacle to happiness, there do exist unhealthy happy people.

What about beauty? Preoccupation with physical appearance also seems to be on the rise, among both men and women. This is probably connected not only with the growing fear of age, but also with the growing obsession with sex. "Obsession" is actually the name of a woman's perfume, alongside "Opium," "Addict," and "Poison."

One fad in advertising aimed at women these days is to call being viewed as beautiful "empowering." The question, I suppose, is what those who are viewed as beautiful are being empowered to do. Apparently, to attract men. I remember a social occasion some years ago. Dinner would be served in a few minutes. Over glasses of wine, the women were exchanging compliments on their appearance. Cora told Kathryn she looked sexy. Kathryn was pleased. Much younger than I am now, I was something of a boor. Something got into me. I turned to Cora.

"Both of you are lovely—"

"Thank you."

"—but what do you mean when you call Kathryn 'sexy'?"

"I mean attractive. Desirable."

"Forgive me if I'm too literal," I answered, "but what desire do you mean?"

"Sexual desire. What else would I mean?"

"So the basis of your compliment is that the way Kathryn looks makes men want to get in bed with her?"

"Sure."

"All men?"

"Sure."

"That's good?"

Cora and Kathryn glanced at each other and laughed. "Is it strange that a woman would want to be desirable?"

"Well, you wouldn't want to have sex with all men, would you?" I asked.

"No," Kathryn said.

"Then why would you want all men to desire to have sex with you?"

"Don't you understand a woman wanting to be beautiful?" asked Cora.

"Sure," I said.

"Well, then?"

"But you didn't speak of beauty. You spoke of sexiness."

"Aren't they the same thing?" they both exclaimed.[9]

As someone more discreet laughingly pointed out to me later, I should have known better than to mix it up at a wine and dinner party. If Socrates and Alcibiades had been there, then maybe. Otherwise, no. He was right.

The fact remains that many women do think this way—and certainly many men do too. But surely the idea of being beautiful and the idea of being able to provoke lust are not the same thing. I am fairly confident that the sculptor who made the Statue of Liberty tried to give her beauty, but I doubt that he intended that men want to bed her. The relationship between beauty and the ability to capture the attention of the other sex can be explained in many other ways too, although we need not settle the issue among the different theories. For example, I have it on reliable feminine authority that a great many women care more about how they look to other women than about how they look to men. According to these informants, the issue in female competition isn't whether male interest matters, but *how* it matters: women are less interested in whether men find their looks appealing than in whether other women *think* men find their looks appealing. By this theory, although some women really are in direct competition for male attention, perhaps just as many or even more are competing over their rank in the society of other females. My feminine informants add that this is a double-edged sword, because women also tend to judge the prettiest women with much greater suspicion—and so, in some contexts, do men.

The notion that bodily loveliness is all gain and no loss is a myth, and the laugh line, "Don't hate me because I'm beautiful!" deserves less mockery than it receives. In certain lines of work, beauty may get a woman through the door, but once through it she may be judged more harshly: coworkers and supervisors wonder whether she got the job just because she was pretty. In courtship, the glamorously beautiful also tend to attract people for the wrong reasons: *Is he pursuing me because he loves me, or only because I look like a good lay?* Speaking of courtship, unattractive people don't really find it much more difficult to get married. They only find it more difficult to marry the most attractive people—and the one whom I love tends to look beautiful to me anyway, even transcendently beautiful.

Preoccupation with beauty operates somewhat differently among men and women. A common observation is that most women care less about how men look than men care about how women look. Male preoccupation with feminine beauty works to the disadvantage of men themselves in two different ways. A man may hold back from pursuing a beautiful and available woman for fear of rejection, mistakenly thinking, *I wouldn't have a chance with her.* Or he may pass over a wonderful woman because he is waiting for "the perfect babe." Neither attitude seems a good formula for happy choice. Some people think the disparity between masculine and feminine interest in the beauty of the opposite sex must be in the genes. Maybe, but this is no reason for fatalism, for what matters is not our predispositions but what we do with them. The courageous person tempers his predisposition to excessive fear, the moderate person his predisposition to excessive pleasure, and the romantically prudent person his predisposition to certain physical types.

If beauty were the path to happiness, then since looks inevitably deteriorate as we age, there shouldn't be any happy old people. There are. Of course the very old may regret the loss of their good looks, but they are usually less obsessed about their looks than the young are. The most fortunate among them have begun to figure out what really matters. Besides, although our health and looks are fleeting and transitory, we rightly think of happiness as something that abides. If I say, "I was happy when I was young and beautiful, but miserable now that I am old and funny to look at," then the truth of the matter is that I was never happy to begin with. For a while, things were going well for me, and now they aren't; that's all. Happiness, in the sense of fulfillment, is not a function of how things are going at the moment, but of the quality and shape of my life.

One of the most important things to be said is almost as commonsensical as the ones we have already been saying, but much more difficult to put in commonsense language because it has to do with our souls. Please understand that I am not using the term "soul" to sneak in assumptions some people would object to as "religious"; I am using it in a much more general sense. By the human soul I mean only the ruling pattern of an embodied human life—that which makes the difference between a human being and a corpse. The usual religious question is not whether we have souls (for obviously our embodied lives have ruling patterns), but whether our souls are immortal (whether these ruling patterns can survive bodily death). At present I am not addressing that question, though it may be important later on.

The point that I want to make is that the normal state of a human being in this life (whether or not it is the only life) is neither a disembodied soul nor a soulless body; we are bodies *united* with souls. A human body without a soul would be a cadaver; if a human soul without a body is possible at all, it would be, at best, diminished.[10] Now the unity of body and soul raises a question: Which one is more important? Although the paradoxical idea that our souls exist for our bodies is not unheard of, the vast majority of human beings in all times and places have thought it is the other way around: that our bodies exist for our souls. The soul is what ennobles this otherwise dead flesh and makes the composite *me*.

If this is true, then something important follows. For if the soul rules, and the body exists for its sake, then the goods of the body are *subordinate* to the goods of the soul. Since happiness is not a subordinate good, but the very summit of good, happiness cannot lie in the goods of the body, so it cannot lie in health or beauty.

To sum up, we have found the view that happiness is identical with bodily health and beauty to be false—but we have also found two grains of truth in it, which explain, perhaps, why so many people think it entirely true.

One of these grains concerns health, for the most extreme suffering does push out all enjoyment. No theory of happiness that denied this fact would deserve much respect. But, in the first place, not all defects in health do push out all enjoyment, for not only are there numerous happy people in rather poor health, but some sick persons have the gift of making the best of their illness; cheerfulness in adversity is rightly and universally praised as a virtue. And in the second place, from the fact that poor health impairs happiness it does not follow that good health *is* happiness, or even that it produces it.

The other grain of truth concerns beauty. As social beings, we do care whether others find us pleasant to look at; we can't help it. One can even put the matter in moral terms, for it is a genuine social duty to try to make our company pleasant to others, and a dirty, slovenly person who takes no care for his appearance is inconsiderate! If it is true that we should take pleasure in the exercise of the virtues, then why not in the exercise of this virtue? But the vice of vanity—and aren't all the vices roots of sorrow?—is not the same thing as the innocent desire to be pleasing to others. It is a *corruption* of that innocent desire, seeking not that we each delight each other, but that I myself be more delightful than all the rest. How right it is for unmarried persons to want to seem persons with whom it would be delightful to be married! But how morbid it is for married persons to want to seem persons with whom it would be more delightful to be married than to the persons to whom the onlookers are married already!

CHAPTER 6

## Could Fame or Sheer Notice Be Happiness?

"It is pleasing to be pointed at with the finger and to have it said, 'There he is.'"[1]

T his chapter is not concerned with whether happiness lies in being admired for good qualities; I take that up in the next. For now, let's consider whether it lies simply in the attention of others. I use the term "fame" for being noticed on a very large scale and the term "infamy" as one of fame's divisions—the fame that accrues to wicked deeds rather than good. If the game is attention, then either kind will do: the more of it, the better.

A naïve person might suppose that the sheer desire for attention, entirely apart from what brings it, is confined to small children. This misconception is easy to understand, since the desire is so conspicuous among them. Sometimes, of course, children seek attention because they want something—a snack, a story, a game, or a cuddle. But sometimes all they want is the attention itself. New parents are often baffled that their little ones may do mischief even with the frank expectation of being scolded or punished for it. Craftier than their elders, these little ones grasp that unfavorable attention is still attention—and for them, attention is the thing. It isn't that they *like* the displeasure of their parents. It's just that that in order to discipline them, their parents have to notice them, and the more the children are noticed, the better they are pleased. Some parents, missing the point entirely, have long talks with their little scoundrels about why their behavior is so naughty. For kids, that's the jackpot.

But isn't being praised or rewarded for *good* behavior attention too? Of course it is. Its disadvantage is that the attention that results from misbehavior is very likely to be much more intense. From the child's point of view it may be a toss-up whether it is better to have a mild pleasure from praise, unmixed with distress, or to have an intense pleasure from a scolding, mixed with sharp distress. Besides, the child never knows whether anyone will notice his good behavior—but he can be pretty sure to be noticed if he is bad. Granted, this sort of motive is most spectacularly on display among children who have been neglected. But to some degree, all children live by it.

But as I said, the motive is not confined to children. In one of his books, Machiavelli criticizes the vile Giovanpagolo Baglioni, tyrant of Perugia, for surrendering his city to Pope Julius II even though, had it come to a fight, Giovanpagolo would have won. Although Machiavelli comments on Giovanpagolo's pusillanimity, his criticism is not precisely that Giovanpagolo was a coward, but that he passed up an opportunity to win eternal fame by committing a dreadful deed: "Giovanpagolo, who thought nothing of incurring the guilt of incest, or of murdering his kinsmen, could not, or more truly durst not, avail himself of a fair occasion to do a deed which all would have admired; which would have won for him a deathless fame...and which would have displayed a greatness far transcending any infamy or danger that could attach to it."

The lesson Machiavelli draws is that if one cannot gain fame through being good, then at least one ought to gain it through being bad. Middle ways are foolish because they bring no fame to anyone.[2] To Machiavelli, it makes sense to give paramount importance to fame, because we crave immortality, but the only immortality we know lies on earth, in being remembered forever, whether for good or for ill.

So small children are not the only ones who think the fact of getting attention may be more important than the means by which one gets it. We don't need the example of Machiavelli to learn this lesson; all history testifies to the extremes to which some have been willing to go for the sake of fame.

Still, there is a difference between an aristocratic age like his and a popular age like ours. Only three centuries ago, when aristocracy had not yet quite died, it was still possible for Joseph Addison to write that "were not this desire of fame very strong, the difficulty of obtaining it, and the danger of losing it when obtained, would be sufficient to deter a man from so vain a pursuit."[3] That was a sharp observation at the time, but it no longer holds in our day, for fame has been largely democratized. Although it is still difficult to attain *enduring* fame, there is no longer a need to do anything spectacular to attain fame of the transitory sort.

Pop artist Andy Warhol famously prophesied in 1968 that "in the future, everyone will be world-famous for fifteen minutes," and the social media have turned his prediction into an aspiration of the masses. Besides, in an age in which many people have no sense of history, exhibit no interest in posterity, and think that death blots out this short life, fifteen minutes of fame may sound pretty good.

Some of the things people do for attention are innocent, or at worst silly, as in the case of the woman who posted a video of herself donning a Chewbacca the Wookie mask and laughing hysterically for several minutes; that one was viewed more than 13 million times[4] and won the lady in the mask a television appearance.[5] A number of other persons found their own fifteen minutes of fame by piggyback-ing on hers, posting videos of themselves doing nothing but *watching* the Chewbacca mask video.

Others are not so innocent. Typical of the vicious sort is the video of a girl in a grocery store opening a carton of ice cream, licking it, and returning it to the freezer case, egged on by the friend who recorded the scene. That one was viewed more than thirteen million times, garnering tens of thousands of retweets and sixty-five thou-sand social media "likes."[6] A "like," in this context, doesn't necessar-ily mean "I liked what she did" but just "I liked watching this." Apparently that's all the motivation it takes, because the ice cream licker was honored by a spate of copycats. Caught, one man said he was sorry, yet boasted to interviewers that his video was viewed more than fifty thousand times during the first twenty-four hours.[7] Some of these copycat incidents seem to have been phony—people feigning sickness and then pretending to lick food or to sneeze or cough on it rather than really doing so. To the perpetrators, however, it makes no difference. For even if only anonymously, and even if only for acts of turpitude, they have been noticed.

Of course not everyone goes to such extremes, but it seems that some people will go to any lengths to have the attention of others. One pop star, whom I resolutely refuse to name, had herself filmed riding a wrecking ball in the nude. Just to leave no doubt as to her intention, at a certain point in the video she is said to have mouthed the words "pay attention to me." Apparently she expected viewers to pay close enough attention to attempt to read her lips. Apparently she was right.

And consider the strange phenomenon of people "famous for being famous," whose lives are followed avidly by millions who have no idea what first catapulted them into public notice. The sheer fact that they are noticed is so interesting to the fans that these enthusiasts reward them with more notice—at least until the fifteen minutes are over. True, part of the public interest in the lives of the famous-for-being-famous is malicious; the crowd is hoping that they will slip and fall. But it would not be nearly as entertaining to see them make fools of themselves were it not for the fact that they are envied. Obviously, such persons are not envied for what they did to burst into the spotlight, since no one remembers what it was. They are envied just for the fact that they are in it.

How well does fame or being noticed stand up against what we understand happiness to be?

We think of happiness as something noble and exalted, but as we have already amply seen, some will lower themselves to any depth for the sake of attention. Complete happiness is incompatible with its opposite, but fame is entirely compatible with misery. Consider the embarrassing spectacle of the pop star who had herself filmed melting down, tearfully but ironically blubbering that she wanted her viewers to leave her alone and stop tormenting her with cruel comments on social media.[8] It is a dreadful thing to live on a public platform, to have no boundaries, to lose the membrane that separates us from the perpetual scrutiny of others.

Happiness is something that endures and is not easily lost. But fame is short-lived. As soon as the onlooker becomes familiar with an entrancing spectacle that seizes his attention, he becomes bored by it and falls out of the trance. Though some people remain famous for a long time, they do so only at a cost, because they must continually feed the restless eyes of the spectators with new things to gaze upon. In fact the attention seeker must not only keep doing new things, but keep finding more conspicuous new things, because the old ones have become stale. It takes more and more to recapture their jaded attention.

Happiness is not at the mercy of others, but fame is utterly dependent on the crowd. It cannot be commanded. He who craves fame puts himself in the absolute power of others and subjects himself to the freaks of their notice. He loses his freedom and makes himself a slave. Happiness is associated with sufficiency; it should leave nothing to be desired. But those who crave fame never think they have enough. Like a shot of vodka, each new burst of attention goes right to the head, but rather than satisfying, its dizzy delight whets the appetite for more, setting the seeker to seek it anew. Moreover, the enjoyment of fame, like the enjoyment of wealth, is never as great as we imagine it will be—and we are much more cast down by the loss of others' attention, or the fear of losing it, than we could ever have been pleased by having it.

But if we do fancy being noticed so rewarding, what generates this fancy? What good thing does notice do for us, or at least seem to do for us? What makes the delusion that fame equals happiness so persuasive? The answer lies in the fact that we are social beings. This point is easy to misunderstand. The fact that we are social does not mean just that we have a social instinct, for in that case the statement that "we want to be noticed because we are social" would be circular. It would be like saying that "we want to be noticed because we want to be noticed." It would explain nothing.

To avoid misunderstanding, it may be helpful to distinguish between the pushes and the pulls of our nature. A *push* is a blind, mechanical cause that we cannot disregard, like the impulse that makes our hearts beat or that makes us breath in and out. A *pull* is something we have some choice about, but to which we do well to pay attention because it directs us toward the fulfillment of our potentialities, including, for humans, our rational potentialities. To see the difference more clearly, consider a cow, which is a social creature, like us, but which, unlike us, is not rational.

The cow is *pushed* by its instincts to herd with other cows. It doesn't know why it herds with them; it just does. By contrast, whether or not we have such things as instincts, we are *pulled* to associate because for our kind of being, the good life is truly a good life only when it can be shared with others. We don't need others just for the reasons the beasts need them, for we also have ends higher than theirs. We wonder about things; we desire to know; we long to know the truth, especially about the greatest things. We rely on others to gain knowledge even more than we rely on them for things that we share with cows. Human life turns out to be a partnership not just in such things as eating and protecting ourselves, as it is among them, but also in finding and living by the truth. A cow does not ask, "What am I?" I do ask it—but I cannot even ask it without also asking, "What are *we*?"

In short, we don't just have an itch to be social; our completion requires it. We are not just pushed toward others by our urges but drawn into fellowship for our fulfillment. Everything concerning life in community has the most penetrating importance to us. But a wholesome human community is a far more subtle and complex thing than a herd of cows, and here is the kick: mutual notice or recognition is one of its subtle and complex necessities.

Not only does being noticed reassure us of our standing in the group, it belongs to the very life of the group. In order to court each other, marry each other, raise young together, build cities together, teach each other, and consider the ultimate questions together, we must notice others and be noticed by them in turn. Otherwise the whole thing grinds down.

The young pop star who had herself filmed taking a nude ride on a wrecking ball was not perverse because she wanted other people to know her, but because in her the normal desire to be known had been raised to an abnormal degree and become a disease of the soul. As we have seen about wealth, about health, and about beauty, so we see about fame or attention: the great thing is not just to satisfy our desires, but to shape and refine them so that they can attain their natural purposes.

Most people are able to see that liking, admiration, and approval are better than sheer attention—and this leads us to our next topic.

CHAPTER 7

## *Could Glory or Praise Be Happiness?*

"The desire of glory is the last infirmity cast off even by the wise."[1]

L et us have done with fame, which is merely being noticed by the many. Now let us consider not only being noticed, but being thought great. Though sometimes called fame, the acclaim of the many is more precisely called glory. We have seen that ultimate happiness does not lie in fame, but could it lie in glory?

Who doesn't find even the admiration of a single person pleasant? The honor and veneration of thousands—especially of those whom we consider qualified to judge us, and especially if we expect their good judgment to persist into future generations—is so gratifying that the very thought of it has the power to stir and elate us.

Mother Teresa of Calcutta is considered great because she secreted herself in the slums to comfort the sick and forgotten with no thought of glory whatsoever. Aside from the saints, however, this sort of glory is the exception; greatness is most often pursued and achieved in the most conspicuous occupations. Statecraft, war, and athletics (which is sublimated war) receive more attention than humble service to the poor. However, the keen desire for glory is also a propulsive motive in medicine, science, entertainment, literature, the arts, and some of the professions.

Some nations have been more notorious for craving glory than others. Augustine remarks that the Roman political class were "greedy of praise": "Glory they most ardently loved: for it they wished to live, for it they did not hesitate to die. Every other desire was repressed by the strength of their passion for that one thing."[2]

Although even the ordinary man may fancy an inscription on his grave, glory is won mostly by achievements considered marvelous. However, because there is something of the dog in most of us, glory can also be awarded for mere pomp and grandeur, the mere trappings of wealth and dominion. In rare cases, in a society that is not altogether corrupt, glory may even be accorded to persons of virtue. More often, though, we exalt persons who have the *appearance* of virtue—or if not of genuine virtue, then at least of the qualities that please us.

Commonly we accord superlative moral character to men just because of the great deeds they have undertaken. This is a mistake, because although those who desire to do good for its own sake will persist in it without acclaim, those who desire acclaim for its own sake will desist from doing good if they have no prospect of fame. That is why Alexander Hamilton remarks,

"Even the love of [glory],[3] the ruling passion of the noblest minds, which would prompt a man to plan and undertake extensive and arduous enterprises for the public benefit, requiring considerable time to mature and perfect them, if he could flatter himself with the prospect of being allowed to finish what he had begun, would, on the contrary, deter him from the undertaking, when he foresaw that he must quit the scene before he could accomplish the work, and must commit that, together with his own reputation, to hands which might be unequal or unfriendly to the task. The most to be expected from the generality of men, in such a situation, is the negative merit of not doing harm, instead of the positive merit of doing good."[4]

For this and for other reasons, on those lucky occasions when we do recognize the ardent desire for glory for glory's sake, we tend to be suspicious of those who have it and to praise those who lack it, or at least those who seem to lack it. Thus it was said of Cato the Elder—whether justly or not—that he preferred to be good rather than seem good, and so the less he pursued glory, the more it pursued him.[5]

Numerous writers, more glib than wise, take the opposite view. They assure us that a bad man can be a great statesman, and that a bad motive can produce a great deed. By a great statesman, they seem to mean someone who possesses the skills of statecraft, and their point is that virtue and skill are not necessarily connected. And of course this is true. A bad man may have skill, and so he may accomplish something that happens to be good—he may enact a good law or win a war that has to be fought. There are many such cases in history.

But if the bad man's motives are flawed, then if it suits his purposes he is just as likely to do something evil. One cannot be *confident* that he will do the right thing. Besides, precisely because his motive is flawed, even when he does intend something good, he is likely to do it in an evil way. Finally, there are some good things he cannot do even if they do chance to coincide with his motives. For example, a bad man cannot successfully promote good character in others, and he will probably injure their character by his example. Besides, no matter what he does, he will lie to you about it.

Augustine has given us the most acute diagnosis of this problem. Although in itself, he says, the craving for glory is a vice, it does impersonate a virtue, and the Roman republic depended on this impersonation for the common good.[6] One way the impersonation worked was that it moved men to suppress lesser vices for glory's sake. Thus, members of the Roman political class who desired glory above all things often suppressed their almost equally strong desire for wealth, contenting themselves with moderate fortunes. The impersonation also spurred such men to great labors for the benefit of the commonwealth. Thus they defeated enemies and reformed constitutions just so that others would honor them for doing so.

The weakness of this cultural policy is that glory can be won by foul means as well as fair. For example, a man may attain high office through a deserved reputation, but he may also attain it through buying votes. So long as he retains some little trace, some little residuum of true virtue, he will use fair means rather than foul to attain glory. However, little by little the craving for glory undermines this little trace of virtue, for the strong desire for glory "breeds several vicious habits in the mind," as Addison says.[7] Once men are willing to use foul means, the desire for glory no longer successfully impersonates a virtue, and the society begins to collapse.

Augustine also explains that whatever the effects of the longing for glory upon the domestic policy of the commonwealth may have been, they were dreadful for the commonwealth's neighbors. For "because it seemed inglorious to serve, but glorious to rule and to command, [the Romans] first earnestly desired to be free, and then to be mistress."[8] In their treatment of other nations they loved justice for the sake of glory, rather than glory for the sake of justice. Consequently, they were not above casting justice overboard when it was inconvenient.[9]

The greed for glory is also self-defeating, because it betrays the ambitious man into acts of vice that in turn may diminish his glory—if not in everyone's judgement, then at least among those best able to judge, the very ones whose acclaim he most covets. In the meantime, fearful that his merits will be overlooked, he will constantly be tempted to boast of his qualities and deprecate the merits of others. This vain habit will expose him to scorn and derision, "and as the world is more apt to find fault than to commend, the boast will probably be censured when the great action that occasioned it is forgotten."[10]

I mentioned in the previous chapter how easy it is in our day to win short-lived fame. Yet it remains terribly hard to win enduring glory for noble deeds. Jonathan Swift remarked that "censure is the tax a man pays to the public for being eminent."[11] One reason is that in any human society, a great many people are incapable of distinguishing between true gold and tinsel. Another is that even if we are capable of distinguishing them, we may not allow ourselves to do so. Why not? Mostly because of cynicism, envy, and petty pride. If we are of a cynical turn of mind, we habitually disbelieve in lofty motives, thinking that everything is done for base ones—and if we are of an envious turn of mind, we deliberately misrepresent or misinterpret the intentions of everyone who attempts something great. We grieve over the merits of others because they make our own seem less, and we magnify our own by belittling theirs. We congratulate ourselves for having such excellent judgment that we can spy out flaws in those whom others admire. If we can convert those others into despisers like ourselves, we think we have done something great. My point is not that these are vices (though they are), but that they make the prognosis very poor for those who love to be praised.

Consider too that if those who deride others lack the faults that they perceive in great men, then they feel elevated just for not having them—and if they do have them, then by finding them in great men, they excuse them in themselves. They may even praise themselves for resembling the elevated persons whom they criticize—even if only in their faults! Besides, as Addison points out, the exposure of the vices and weaknesses of persons commonly thought to be of purer alloy is so delightful that whoever does expose them wins a sort of glory of his own. Perhaps the crowd admires the author of the exposé for being so clever that he can ridicule someone who would have seemed immune to ridicule. Or perhaps it enjoys a kind of revenge in taking down someone so high.[12]

In an age like ours, which makes a fetish of equality, such motives are intensified. Persons of distinguished qualities seem despicable just because they are raised above others. True, we may praise moderate virtue, but we tend to view great virtue itself as a sort of vice. In any case, most people are readier to criticize a person's faults than to admire his merits—except, of course, for flatterers, whose praises please only fools.

In any case it isn't difficult to find faults in a person who craves glory. One reason is that the craving for glory is likely to lead him into other faults. Besides, he is paying so much attention to all the things he has to do to attain glory that he forgets to guard whatever little portion of virtue he began with. On top of that, any slip on his part is more conspicuous than the same slip would be in those regarded as nobodies—partly because he is under constant public inspection, and partly because the fault seems so out of keeping with the rest of his perceived character. The moment his slip is espied, onlookers who may have thought him incapable of grave fault now begin to wonder what other faults he is hiding. If his discovered faults seem great enough, they overshadow his good qualities—and there will always be legions who have something to gain from *making* them seem great.

The previous chapter's observations about the brevity of fame apply to glory too. Everyone who remembers the renowned person will soon die. Even in the unlikely event that a few moldy history books preserve his memory, the people of the future will be taken up with the affairs of their own times, scarcely giving a thought to the events and personages of ours. Even if the person who seeks glory is satisfied to be praised in his own lifetime, he will be equally disappointed, for acclaim is a mayfly and whoever seeks it must always be doing still greater things to keep it aflutter. Worse, as though he were a cast-off lover, the crowd may reserve its greatest derision for someone whom it once admired but no longer does.

To the glory-monger, this reversal of fortune is intolerable. However intoxicating the admiration of the many may be, their contempt is an agony hardly to be borne—and if the many did once think him great, his torment is keener yet, for the memory of their former praise will lance into his bowels like a razor. In fact, a person who falls from receiving glory is cast down much further than someone who falls from merely receiving attention. For anyone who can be made dizzy with praise can be crushed by derision, and the ambitious man shrivels inwardly if he falls the least bit short of the praise that he expected or thinks he deserves. It will almost always fall short, too, because, as Addison reminds us, few people ever think as well of us as we think of ourselves.[13]

So like the seeker of sheer attention, so too the seeker of glory never thinks he has enough—and to win the portion he does have, he puts himself in the power of others. In fact, he puts himself *most* in the power of those who are *least* able to judge his achievements, and who have the greatest motives to throw him down.

Finally, though it has often been remarked that the most talented crave glory the most, the most virtuous crave it the least. Looking down on the petty criticisms and plaudits of the crowd, they stand above its sneers and cheers. Those who are best able to appreciate a truly noble achievement understand this characteristic of great men—and from those who most urgently desire their approval, they withhold it.

For all these reasons, glory is unsatisfying, and the greater the desire for glory, the more likely it is to defeat itself. So although it is only to be expected that we would desire the approval of our fellows, ultimate happiness must lie elsewhere.

# CHAPTER 8

# Could Loving or Esteeming Ourselves Be Happiness?

"As I bent down to look, just opposite
A shape within the wat'ry gleam appear'd,
Bending to look on me."[1]

I f happiness doesn't lie in the esteem of others, could it be that it lies in esteeming ourselves?

The accumulated common sense of centuries says no. Self-respect isn't the key to living well, but its result. In the 1970s, though, psychologists and educators began arguing that this ancient common sense is dead wrong. On the Left, their argument found support in the politics of identity and in the crusade for "politically correct" language that seeks to abolish any chance that anyone might ever be offended (except, of course, conservatives). On the Right, it found support in the version of libertarianism that preaches "the virtue of selfishness" and dotes on the novels of Ayn Rand.[2]

Since that time, boosting self-esteem has been touted as the solution to high crime rates, drug abuse, teen pregnancy, domestic violence, poor learning in schools, unemployment, abuse of the environment, and even unbalanced state government budgets.[3] The idea is that these problems result from having a poor self-image, and people just need to learn to feel good about themselves. One writer comments, "The very idea that high self-esteem could have bad consequences strikes some people as startling."[4] Though he penned these words a quarter of a century ago (which in our era seems much longer), the observation is as true as ever.

The experiment began with children. Rather than simply reassuring little ones of their love and praising them when they did well, adults began telling them things like, "You're amazing just being yourself!" At one elementary school, a banner over the boys' room mirror announced, "You are now looking at one of the most special people in the whole wide world!"[5] Kindergarteners were taught to sing "I am special, I am special, look at me"[6]—as though they didn't already want to be seen. Some school districts switched to marking errors with purple or green ink because red, they thought, was discouraging; never mind that changing the ink in the correction pens would merely change the discouraging color. Some teachers were taught to praise even wrong answers. On athletic field days, children were often awarded ribbons for every place, even last, and the ribbon colors were scrambled after each event.

The movement soon gained allies among the writers of children's books. One little tome urges tots to "say these words three times with pride: I'm lovable. I'm lovable. I'm lovable."[7] Wouldn't it be better to love them? The preface to another book declares that its goal is to show children that "the key to feeling good is liking yourself *because you are you*."[8] Should a boy like himself when he is hitting his sister? In yet another, a mother tells her toddler that even when he was too small to speak, "all of your tininess couldn't disguise a heart so enormous and wild and wise."[9] It is one thing for a mother to encourage her wee bairn by assuring him how much she loves him and *hopes* he will be wise (if not wild). It hardly seems likely to encourage him to acquire wisdom to tell him that he is already wise. Persons of the

Christian faith do not even make such an extravagant claim about the child Jesus, who is said to have *grown* in wisdom and stature.[10]

Some psychologists are still on the boat. Confronted with rising scores on the Narcissistic Personality Inventory, they now argue that a little narcissism may be good for you.[11] The fallacy in the idea of "normal narcissism" is subtle. True, everyone alive is somewhere on the narcissism scale—everyone would have to be, since scales of this kind are *designed* to put everyone somewhere on them, just as thermometers are designed to give even ice cubes a temperature. But from the fact that everyone may need *some* of the qualities that narcissists have *too much* of (such as confidence), it doesn't follow that everyone needs to be *somewhat narcissistic*; narcissism is a personality disorder. To deny this fact betrays ignorance of the age-old insight that excellence of character lies in a mean. Consider courage, which isn't high spirit per se, but habitually having the right amount of high spirit for the circumstances. Habitually having too little is cowardice, and habitually having too much is rashness. It is just as foolish to call appropriate confidence "normal narcissism" as it would be to call courage "normal rashness."

At length, other psychologists have come to realize that the claims of the self-esteem movement are overblown. According to Roy F. Baumeister, who was converted only reluctantly, research shows that high self-esteem does not improve performance at work, make relationships better, reduce violence or bullying, or deter cheating, stealing, drug abuse, or early sex: "In short, despite the enthusiastic embrace of self-esteem, we found that it conferred only two benefits. It feels good and it supports initiative. Those are nice, but they are far less than we had once hoped for."[12]

Indeed. Pleasant feelings can coexist with an objectively miserable life; even the dope addict feels good while he is high. And if we encourage initiative by persuading people that they are more capable than they are, then we are setting them up for a fall. Self-esteem can even backfire. A team of psychologists found that students pulling grades of C and D did *worse* than the control group, not better, after teachers labored to boost their self-esteem.[13]

Persons with inflated self-regard also inflict costs on those around them. A psychologist who asked people to rank both themselves and others in a group found that self-aggrandizers did make good first impressions—others ranked them as especially agreeable, well-adjusted, and competent. But after some weeks, they dropped to the bottom of the rankings.[14] Two other psychologists summarize, "God's gift to the world can be hard to live with."[15]

Yet the train barrels on. Self-esteem scores have risen over the recent decades, while achievement scores have dropped, and psychopathology is on the increase. Interestingly, American kids are more confident than ever before that they outperform their foreign peers—though actually they are falling further behind.[16]

Pop music is very big on self-esteem these days. In a casual survey, I count five variations on the theme:

*Variation 1: I Love Myself.* Not long after the self-esteem movement began, Whitney Houston crooned "Learning to love yourself, it is the greatest love of all."[17] Thirty-five years later, Meghan Trainor simplified the argument: "I love me, I love me, I don't know about you, but baby I love me, now everybody say, hey-hey-hey, oh, hey-hey-hey, I love me."[18]

*Variation 2: I'm Better Than Everyone Else.* Sia chants, "I'm free to be the greatest...ay, I am the truth, ay, I am the wisdom of the fallen, I'm the youth, ay, I am the greatest."[19] Rivers Cuomo proclaims, "I am the greatest man that ever lived, I was born to give (I was born to give), I am the greatest man that ever lived, oh, radioactive."[20]

*Variation 3: I Don't Need Anyone.* Leading the pack is Meghan Trainor again: "I can't help lovin' myself, and I don't need nobody else, nuh uh, if I was you, I'd wanna be me too."[21] Ally Brooke agrees: "If I'm gonna love someone (one), I'm just gonna love myself (self), I already know I'm fabulous, I don't need no one else (no one else)."[22]

*Variation 4: I don't have any flaws.* Exhibit A is Christina Aguilera, who bluntly declares, "I am beautiful in every single way."[23] In a sort of limerick, India Arie elaborates: "Every freckle on my face is where it's supposed to be, and I know my creator didn't make no mistakes on me, my feet, my thighs, my lips, my eyes, I'm lovin' what I see."[24] Lady Gaga is sure she's perfect because her mother told her so: "My mama told me when I was young, we are all born superstars.... 'There's nothing wrong with loving who you are,' she said, 'cause he made you perfect, babe.'"[25]

*Variation 5: I'm not sure I believe all this, but I'm desperately trying to.* Typical of this variation is a song of Alessia Cara. At first she seems only to be boasting: "I'm a million trick pony, the number one and only, on a scale of 1 to 10, I'm at 11 (okay, okay)." As she continues, the boast reveals itself as a device for propping up a fragile sense of self: "Fake it until I make it ring true, one day I'mma be better at feelin' cool, yeah, fake it until I make it ring true, hey, one day I'mma be better at feelin' like a million trick pony."[26]

The interesting thing isn't that so many singers would sing such lyrics, but that so many listeners would want to hear them. Music critics describe such songs as empowering—the same gimmick some beauty merchants use. That sort of empowerment, however, may be very disempowering. For if to get out of my funk I have to believe that I am "practically perfect in every way," then any little failure may threaten my self-image and cast me back down.

It is not hard to see that something is wrong here. But since believable errors contain distorted images of truths, let's see what is true in the notion of self-esteem.

If I have behaved despicably, I should not admire myself, and the best thing I can do for myself is humbly accept what's coming to me. Yet there is a difference between liking and loving. I should always love myself in the sense of desiring for myself what is good and avoiding what is evil. Even the command to love others assumes self-love: The wording of the precept is "you shall love your neighbor *as yourself*."[27] Traditionally, this was not understood to be about how *much* we love our neighbors, but about *how* we love them: we should love them in the same way that we love ourselves.

This teaching was called the "order of love." And what did it say about how we *should* love ourselves and others? Three things:

- Just as we genuinely wish ourselves well, so we should not love others just for our own gain or pleasure, but genuinely wish them well.
- Just as we will for ourselves only true and not false or illusory goods, so we should will for others only true and not false or illusory goods.
- Just as our love for ourselves should be rooted in loving God, so our love for them should be rooted in loving God.[28]

In our time, the third is usually the sticking point. I will not consider even whether there is a God until later in the book, but we can understand the third point even while putting that question off. Think of the argument as an "if-then." Desiring my own good requires desiring my highest good. *If* my highest good is God—a point we are not yet investigating—then loving myself well involves loving God more.

But whatever the highest good is, it cannot be me. The person for whom I desire the supreme good—myself—must be different than the good that I desire for him. I can no more be my own god than I can pull myself up by the hair. Happiness cannot be self-esteem.

# CHAPTER 9

# Could Power or Responsibility Be Happiness?

"I put for a general inclination of all mankind, a perpetual
and restless desire of Power after power, that ceaseth
only in Death."[1]

Writing almost five centuries ago, the first theorist of power, Thomas Hobbes, gave the most general definition of it: "The power of a màn...is his present means, to obtain some future apparent good."[2] Whatever I can use to get something I think good—whether or not it really is good—that's power.

This definition takes in a lot of territory. In the first place, says Hobbes, the union of different powers is power. Friends and helpers are power, because their strengths are united with ours. Wealth, used generously, is power, because it attracts friends and helpers. The reputation for power is power. Anything that makes a man beloved or feared by many people is power, including the mere reputation of loving them. The reputation for prudence is power. Eloquence is power, because it imitates prudence. Success is power, because it produces a reputation for prudence—or at least a reputation for good luck—so that others come either to fear or to rely on the successful person. Privileges are power. Bodily beauty is power. For those who already have power, geniality is an increase in power. Finally, says Hobbes, practical knowledge is power—for instance knowing how to make instruments of war and defense.

But the Hobbesian definition is too broad for our purposes. Everyone wants to be able to obtain what seems good, but the mere desire for the ability to obtain it is not what we ordinarily mean by the love of power. I will use the term "power" only for the means of ruling, directing, or strongly influencing others.

Even taken in this more limited sense, desire for power is universal. In an authoritarian regime, few people admit to desiring power because doing so will get them in trouble with those who do have power—but they desire it. In a republic or supposed republic, few admit to the desire because they associate it with dictators and conquerors—yet they readily admit the desire to be "administrators," join "management," learn "leadership," enter "public service," be "guides," "motivate team members," or have "broader responsibilities." If someone says he wants to "rule," we think he is a bad fellow, but if he expresses a need for "empowerment," has "ambition," or aspires to "leadership," we think he is a fine one.

Such quirks of language are not always self-deceptions. At the bottom of them may be a reasonable wish to distinguish between excessive power and the authority that is appropriate to one's calling and station in life. Businessmen may want authority to direct their own enterprises, without wishing to run schools or the Church. Teachers may want authority to teach their students, without wishing to control their lives. Parents may guard their authority over their children for the children's own good, without wishing for tyranny over them or dominion over other children. In each of these little realms, the right kind of power can be exercised moderately and humbly, even if some people overreach.

Thus, taking into account the fact that people may desire power only of certain kinds, in certain degrees, and in certain settings, and that they may desire it even if they defer to superior authority in others, it seems that everyone wants some power, and everyone is convinced that having it has something to do with his happiness. But in every society, some people draw the more ambitious conclusion that if some power is good, more is better, and if some kinds are good, all kinds are. Whether or not they admit it to themselves, these people view power over others as the key to their happiness.

Could they be right?

Not all motives for unlimited power concern us here. Some seek power to be admired, but we have already considered glory. Some seek it to prop up their egos, but we have already considered self-esteem. Some seek it for sufficiency, but we have already considered wealth, which is closely akin. However, we do need to consider two other motives. For some seek power in order to cut the world to a pattern of their choice: this is the totalitarian impulse. And others seek power for its own sake: they want the sheer exaltation of dominion.

Sometimes we encounter these motives unmixed and straight from the bottle. More often they are disguised by other motives. For example, when Luke Day, one of the leading spirits of Shays' Rebellion, harangued his men, he flavored the lust for power with the desire for liberty and piety: "My boys, you are going to fight for liberty. If you wish to know what liberty is, I will tell you. It is for every man to do what he pleases, *to make other folks do as you please to have them,* and to keep folks from serving the devil" (emphasis added).[3]

Although the ancients were keenly aware of the hunger for power, they did not clearly distinguish the hunger for power in itself from either of these other two motives. As to the former motive, the desire to reshape the world according to their desires, they had plenty of experience of tyranny, but totalitarianism was unknown to them; the ancient tyrant wasn't trying to remake the world, but to be the top dog. As to the latter motive, the sheer exaltation of dominion, they knew that some people crave power, but they tended to think that everyone who does so craves it to get something else, such as gold, glory, or girls. In fact, this view was the premise for one of their *critiques* of the idea that happiness lies in power: that since nobody does want power for itself, what we really want must be something else! This seems mistaken, for both the totalizing impulse and the motive of pure aggrandizement seem real.

Either of these two motives may make itself known just as easily in a small setting as in a large. The former, for example, may take the form of a suffocating demand for political correctness at the office and the latter in the petty tyranny of an overbearing boss. However, the inherent tendency of both motives is to seek a wider and wider scope of action. Now when someone seeks a particular kind of power for a limited and particular reason—in business, in teaching, in raising children—there comes a point at which he can say "I have what I need for my work." But when someone seeks power for either the totalizing or the aggrandizing motive, that point is never reached. He always wants more.

Obviously, although all these considerations give us reason to think that some people will suffer if *others* desire power in excess, none of these considerations will deter those who think power the key to their own happiness. If I think it is the key, there is not much point in telling me, "Stop trying to be happy, because it may make others unhappy." But are there reasons to think that excessive power *won't* make me happy?

Yes, there are many. Let's consider some of the most important.

In the first place, excessive power deprives me of some of the greatest consolations of human life. Most obviously, it causes me to forfeit all confidence in friendship. How can I ever know that my companions are true friends, and not flatterers and hangers-on? How can I know they wouldn't desert me the moment I fell from my perch?

In the second place, those who seem to have the greatest power have, in another sense, the least. This is why, when Boethius has been imprisoned by the king, Lady Philosophy comforts him, "Do you count him to possess power whom you see to wish what he cannot bring to pass? Do you count him to possess power who encompasses himself with a body-guard, who fears those he terrifies more than they fear him, who, to keep up the semblance of power, is himself at the mercy of his slaves?"[4] The danger of having too much power lies not only in assassins but also in colleagues, for "power endures no partner"[5]—at least not if they crave it as an end in itself. So it is that those at the bottom are at risk of oppression from those who have power; those who have power are in yet greater peril from those who have more; and those with the greatest power are in the gravest and most continuous danger of all. In a culture of power-seeking, everyone is afraid all the time. Such considerations ought to give pause even to sociopaths.

In the third place—and this time I am not speaking to sociopaths—unlimited power is a moral danger. Even most people who do seek it tell themselves at first, "But I will also be just." The very fact that we promise this to ourselves is a clue that in itself, power is at best an incomplete good. The problem is that if we think power the greatest good, then all such other considerations are eventually pushed aside.

Why should that be true? Everyone has heard Lord Acton's maxim that "power tends to corrupt, and absolute power corrupts absolutely."[6] Less well known, but I think more chilling, is an insight best put by an early American statesman who wrote under the pseudonym "Brutus."[7] Fearing that the proposed Constitution might give men more power than is good for them, Brutus alludes to an incident from Syrian history. Benhadad, the Syrian king, is gravely ill. Learning that Elisha, considered a prophet, has come to the capital, he sends his subordinate Hazael to inquire whether he will recover. Elisha instructs Hazael to tell the king that the illness will not kill him—*but he also informs Hazael that the king will die.*

At this point, Elisha gazes upon Hazael until Hazael is ashamed—and then Elisha weeps. Hazael, using the humble address customary in speaking to a superior, asks, "Why does my lord weep?" Elisha replies, "Because I know the evil that you will do to the people of Israel; you will set on fire their fortresses, and you will slay their young men with the sword, and dash in pieces their little ones, and rip up their women with child." Astonished, calling himself a mere dog, a servant of power rather than a ruler, Hazael asks how he could commit such enormities. Elisha answers simply, "The Lord has shown me that you are to be king over Syria."

And so it is. Hazael gives Benhadad the message, but the next day he suffocates the king and becomes king in his place. All the days of his reign he oppresses Elisha's people. Despite his own disbelief that he could be the man and commit the atrocities that Elisha had foretold, thus he becomes and thus he does.

Brutus concludes, "Men are apt to be deceived both with respect to their own dispositions and those of others." It isn't just that power makes us worse than we were at the beginning. Power also gives us the opportunity to act out the vices we already possess without knowing, bringing to the surface faults we would have condemned, but that lurk in our hearts unsuspected.[8]

Who then is truly most powerful? The classical answer is, "He who has power over himself."[9] But who has most power over himself?

Taken literally, isn't it absurd to speak of ruling myself? How can the same thing—me—be both ruler and ruled? Taken as intended, though, the idea is perfectly reasonable. It means that I have more than one element within me, and I identify with the one that is highest and best. Thus, if my noblest element subordinates and directs the baser ones, I am said to rule myself—but if my baser elements subordinate and direct the noblest one, I am said to be a slave. In this traditional view, our highest and best element is rightly said to be reason. Our baser ones are our appetites, including the desire for power. These appetites are like a horse that wants to run but doesn't know where to go; we need to have them, but they cannot direct themselves properly. And the man who is ruled by his appetite for power is as much a slave as a man who is ruled by his lust, by his anger, or by his belly. Instead of riding the horse, he is letting the horse ride him.

If we are confused about this today, the blame is largely due to David Hume, who wrote in the eighteenth century, "Reason is, and ought only to be the slave of the passions, and can never pretend to any other office than to serve and obey them."[10] Hume's view has been enormously influential. But he was cheating. His notion seemed plausible only because he first defined all impulses that affect the will as passions—and then said that only passions can affect the will!

We can disregard such circularities. If the mind cannot motivate the will independently of the appetites, then how is it that it can stand in judgment upon them? For doesn't it? Don't we sometimes say, "I don't want that, but I ought to," and whip ourselves up to desire it? And don't we sometimes say, "I want that very much, but I shouldn't," and hold the appetite down?

Seneca wrote, "Excessive power wants power beyond its power."[11] What lies behind this craving? Power makes us think our reach unlimited. Could it be, then, that the longing for power is a mask for the longing for an infinite good?

I do not dismiss the question of whether desiring an infinite good makes sense; we will return to that deeply serious puzzle later in the book. For now suffice it to say that all *human* power is limited—and the infinite cannot be found in the frangible and finite.

To conclude: Depending on how I am situated in life, I do need certain amounts of certain kinds of power; everyone does. However, my happiness lies not so much in power itself as in using it for good in my station and calling. I may have power, yet lack many things that I need. Too much power may even endanger these things, and the retention of power is not ultimately in my control.

At most I should seek power to direct my own proper affairs and to protect them against others. Desiring dominion over the proper affairs of others is folly. If rule does fall to me—for human beings need laws, and someone must rule—then I should dare exercise rule only to protect the proper powers of the governed over their own affairs, not to usurp them. All of this requires the direction of the virtues—not least of these, humility and justice.

# CHAPTER 10

## Could Pleasure or Delight Be Happiness?

"Stranger, this is a good place to stay: Here pleasure is the highest good."[1]

"I feel it, woohoo.
I feel it, woohoo."[2]

I won't take up the question of whether happiness is something we feel until a later chapter. But if it is a feeling, what other feeling but pleasure could it be? No one would suppose that, say, anger, disappointment, grief, indignation, or stomach-ache is happiness. In addition, happiness is something we seek for its own sake, and who would ever think we seek pleasure for the sake of something else?

But something is fishy here. Philosophers have a name for it: the hedonistic paradox. Pursued for its own sake, pleasure ceases to please. Burned-out pleasure seekers find themselves asking each other, "Are we having fun yet?" Not that amusements don't have their place! As one classical writer remarked, sometimes it is necessary to relax the tension on the bow, lest it break.[3] But a lifetime of amusements would be unendurable; imagine an eternity trapped in Disney World. One may think the prospect is dreadful only because Disney World is so jejune, but taken too far, all amusements are jejune.

Besides, it is impossible to consume all of life in amusements. Anyone who tried to do so would have to go to endless pains just to arrange them and in the end would have less fun than those who are content to take them as they come.

Why does pleasure pall, anyway? Why does fun lose its savor? Because pleasure is the enjoyment of some other good or apparent good. In doing things with my friend, I enjoy friendship. In learning something, I delight in discovery. In reading to my child, I cherish her love of the story. Do I seek friendship, discovery, or reading to my child so that I will have enjoyment? It is mostly the other way around: I seek these things because they are good. Because they are good, I enjoy them, and the enjoyment of them is pleasure. If we pursue what is good as the goal of our actions, pleasure comes as a side effect—but if we pursue pleasure itself as the goal, it becomes tedious.

Hedonists get this backwards. Rather than viewing pleasure as repose in whatever is good, they view pleasure itself as the good—in fact, as the only good there is. From this point of view, a man does not really cherish his wife for her own sake; he cherishes only the pleasure he gets from her. It follows from this theory that if there were a way to have the pleasure of one's wife without the wife, then that would be just as good, or even better. As some think.

Those who do think pleasure is happiness, but refuse to resign themselves to boredom, find that they must turn to more and more extreme amusements to banish it. Before long they find themselves crossing boundaries that they had not intended to cross. In our day of one-click internet searches, perhaps the most conspicuous example, especially among men, is pornography. In the beginning a man may delight merely in viewing the undraped bodies of beautiful women. Soon, perhaps to his surprise, he becomes jaded; mere unclad shapeliness loses its power to arouse him. Consequently he turns to more and more perverse forms of pornography. "Horror is the very spice of his craving. It is ugliness itself that becomes, in the end, the goal of his lechery."[4] And soon even this is not enough.

The illusion that happiness lies in pleasure is easy to dispel. I used to ask my students whether they would be willing to give up their real lives for simulated lives in an experience tank. By some *Matrix*-like witchery, they would *seem* to have perfect friends, *seem* to have perfect knowledge, *seem* to have perfect love, *seem* to have perfect jobs, *seem* to know God, and so on. Thus they would have the pleasure of thinking that they had these things, but all without the trouble of having them. I asked, "Would you trade your life for that one?" Most of my students declined, saying, "It wouldn't be real." Intuitively they grasped that sensations of reality are not the same thing as reality itself, and that pleasure is repose in good, rather than being the good itself.

But a few students did choose the simulation. They said that so long as they didn't know that the experiences weren't real, they would be *just as good* as real—and if they were more pleasurable, *even better!* I should have known better than to suggest that particular thought experiment, because we don't have resources for thinking clearly about things that can't happen. Once I realized that, I changed the scenario to something that *can* happen, removing the confusing fictional element of simulated experience. This time I explained that according to neurophysiologists—and this is true—the brain contains a pleasure center that can be stimulated electrically. Rats, offered a choice between eating and pushing a lever that stimulates the pleasure center, will push it continuously, pleasantly starving themselves to death. I asked: Suppose you were offered the possibility of being strapped to a gurney for the rest of your natural life, provided with all necessary nutrients intravenously, and kept just conscious enough to be fully aware, without distraction, of constant,

ecstatic pleasure at maximum intensity through electrical stimula-
tion of the brain. *Now* would you trade your life for that one? This
time hardly anyone would; in most groups, no one would.

Yet if complete fulfillment really does lie in pleasure, shouldn't
they have? I don't think their final choice was mistaken. I think it
means that at some level, they knew that complete fulfillment does
*not* lie in pleasure. Even among young people, who pursue pleasure
with particular relentlessness, the confusion between happiness and
pleasure withers in the glare of clear thought.

At least with my students it withered as a theory. Whether it
withered in practice—in the way that they conducted their lives—is
more difficult for a teacher to know.

We touched on another reason for thinking that happiness is
different from pleasure in one of the early chapters. For happiness is
inconsistent with unhappiness; the jar cannot be both full and partly
empty. So if pleasure is the same as happiness, pleasure must be also
be inconsistent with displeasure. But it isn't; the two experiences are
co-possible. In fact, pleasure may even depend on pain, and I am not
thinking of masochists: For instance, as Socrates pointed out, I experience the pleasure of scratching only so long as I itch. The moment
the itching ends, so does the pleasure of ending it. We may take itching as a metaphor for all those appetites it is pleasant to scratch. So
if happiness really were the same as pleasure, then the best possible
condition would be to itch intensely and continuously, just so that
we can enjoy intense and continuous scratching.

This is such a dreadful condition that Dante pictures it as one of
the punishments in hell, where he says of two alchemists, "spotted
from head to foot with scabby crusts,"

> I've not seen a currycomb so fast
> Scrubbed by the stableboy whose master's coming,

Or by one waked against his will to hurry,
As did each soul rake himself with the bite
Of fingernails in the great maddening itch.[5]

Occasionally someone says to me that the prospect of continual itching and continual scratching is not dreadful at all. As one of my students pointed out, beer drinkers eat salted peanuts to increase their thirst. Yes, of course, but their reason for increasing their thirst is not to have the pleasure of quenching it, but to be thirsty enough to bring themselves to drink enough to get drunk. For beer is a heavy drink, and apart from the pleasure of intoxication, drinking one beer after another is unpleasant. By making themselves thirsty, they offset that displeasure so that they can enjoy their drunkenness without distraction.

Closely allied with the idea that happiness lies in pleasure is the idea touted by so-called "positive psychologists" that happiness lies in "positive emotions." They suggest ways to have more of the positive and fewer of the negative.[6] But surely there is a confusion here, too. No emotion is always good to have, and none is always bad; it depends. For example, although these psychologists classify sexual pleasure as a positive emotion, it would not be a happy thing to pursue it by neglecting one's wife and consorting with prostitutes. They classify disgust as a negative emotion, yet even they admit that we need to be and ought to be disgusted by such things as cruelty, dishonesty, and boorishness. But if no particular emotion is always bad or good, then isn't the very distinction between positive and negative emotions misleading? What *are* always good, in contrast, are virtues—if we have them—and they direct us to have the right emotions, toward the right persons, in the right ways, on the right occasions, and for the right reasons.

The view of virtue that I have just expressed arouses fierce opposition, for one of the axioms of the therapeutic culture is that we aren't responsible for our emotions and desires. We've all heard the mantras:

*Feelings are neither right nor wrong. They just are.*
*I can't help how I feel; I just do.*
*How I feel is who I am.*

It's true that we can't shut off unwanted feelings like a switch, and it's also true that the very effort of trying to suppress them can stir them up. Even so, our control over our inward life is much greater than we like to admit. Although I may not be able to keep an unwanted guest from entering the house of my mind, or to force her outside after she has entered it, nothing compels me to ask her in. Nor am I compelled to sit down and admire her, to enjoy her attentions, or to invite her to play with my imagination. If I ignore her and go about my business, she will eventually leave my mind on her own—but if I pet her, say, "Don't go yet," and tell her what a lovely feeling she is, she will return another day in power, and that day she will burn down the house. It is comforting to tell ourselves that only our actions matter and not our feelings. But feelings tend to pass into actions.

The false notion that we are helpless in the face of our feelings is deeply ensconced in popular music, usually in connection with the pleasures and pains of love. The singer is said to be chained or enslaved to love; he begs to be set free; he loves someone inappropriate, but asks, "What else can I do?" Well, by that time the horse has escaped from the barn—but had he acted earlier, he could have done quite a bit. This is because though the metaphor of "falling" suggests something inevitable, there is an element of planning even in falling in love. The more time I spend with someone, the more likely I am to fall in love with her. The best way to avoid falling in love with an inappropriate person is to decide ahead of time which sorts of persons are appropriate and spend time only with them.

The lesson to be drawn is that happiness has far less to do with pleasure than it has to do with what we teach ourselves to find pleasurable and painful. Teaching ourselves well is hard work, but we are not mere catspaws of our feelings.

The insight just expressed is an ancient one, and throughout this chapter I have alluded to the insights of the classical thinkers. However, I do not mean to suggest that all of their arguments are persuasive. Commonly they suggest another problem with confusing happiness with pleasure: pleasures tend to be associated with pains—gluttony with gout, drunkenness with hangovers, venery with disease and wrecked families—and all of them with deterioration of the faculties both bodily and intellectual. So far, so good. Sometimes, though, they suggest that perhaps an exception can be made for purely intellectual pleasures. So could happiness lie in *those* feelings?

Now it is true that there is no such thing as a hangover from thinking too much! On the other hand, it is far from true that intellectual activity can bring only pleasure and not pain. Suppose I neglect my family to work out the argument of this book, or that I become depressed from contemplating the fact that not enough people are reading it!

But of course the classical thinkers knew this. What they really had in mind was that human happiness must somehow be connected with the highest activity of the highest human power, which is reason. Is there any object of contemplation that *cannot* be pursued to our harm? I return to this question later in the book. But whether happiness lies in some use of reason is really a different question from whether it lies in pleasant feelings, and I think we now have enough information to settle that question.

In brief: No, it doesn't. Pleasure pleases, but pleasure also palls. In itself it is a grace note, an ornament to something that is truly good; it is the experience of enjoying and resting in that good. We must discern the difference between good and evil, we must learn to take pleasure in true goods rather than in evils that impersonate good, and we must acquire the disciplines of spirit that make doing so possible. At first these disciplines are painful, but after a certain point, like the rhythm of a syncopated passage in a song, they become second nature—not easy, perhaps, but a source of enjoyment in themselves.

So pleasure weaves in and out, around and about our pursuit of the goods of life. Its chord thrums through happiness; its chant proclaims its thrill. But pleasure is not the very meaning of happiness, and to think that it is leads to ruin.

# CHAPTER 11

# Could Painlessness or Annihilation Be Happiness?

"The palsied universe lies before us a leper."[1]

I hope the reader isn't getting tired of anecdotes about students. You can see where they come from; I spend more time with my students than with anyone else except my wife and family. Increasing the risk of boredom, I recycle some of my stories, and the one I am about to tell has appeared in other places. Perhaps the reader will be lucky enough not have come across it.

I used to lead my students through an exercise that parallels an argument in one of Aristotle's classic works.[2] Like him, I asked "What is happiness?" Like his students, my students used to give answers such as "pleasure," "friendship," and "wealth" (though they called wealth "success"). Like him, I encouraged the students to scrutinize each of these common answers more deeply—using the same method as this book. In recent years, however, the exercise has started to fail. On one occasion when I asked my students, "What is happiness?" the first half dozen all gave versions of the answer, "Nothing but freedom from pain and suffering." The negative so filled their minds that they were unable to suggest anything positive that happiness might be.

It is easy to see why someone who is often keenly unhappy might have lost the ability to imagine anything better than freedom from sadness and hurt. And it is certainly true that a person consumed by pain and suffering cannot be called happy. But between those truths and the idea that happiness is nothing but the absence of pain and suffering, however, is a very great distance indeed.

My guess is that most of my students have lived all their young lives in pursuit of pleasure—as the young generally do—but with less restraint from our crumbling conventions than the young have tended to experience in previous generations. Consequently, the hedonistic paradox, which usually kicks in only after we have grown longer in the tooth, has already hit them. He who makes pleasure the object of his life hasn't usually got much of it, but only a basket of displeasures. Although my students don't formulate the paradox explicitly, I suspect that they feel it in their bones.

In the last chapter we saw that on the far side of the paradox lies the insight that pleasure comes as a byproduct of pursuing what is good in itself. Not many of my students get to the far side. Their parents, friends, and teachers, led on by the mighty enchanters of culture, blare in their ears that pleasure simply *is* happiness, simply *is* the good in itself. Living by this rule leads to sorrow. Consequently, their first cheerful idea, that happiness is pleasure, suffers a dark transmutation into the equally naïve but morbid idea that happiness is just absence of pain. And that is what they say in my classroom. Not many of them look happy. Each year they have less sense of humor. Many show signs of exhaustion. Though they have never heard of Schopenhauer, they are intuitive Schopenhauerians. Although they may say things such as "I am having an awesome life!"—as one of them did in a course survey—they grow weary in the midst of excitements.

One sympathizes. To a person who is beginning to experience hedonistic burnout, freedom from pain might seem pretty good. Perhaps he used to think he could have pleasure all the time; now he finds that the quest for it leaves him dismayed. But rather than questioning his initial premise "Happiness is pleasure," he merely scales back his hopes. He no longer demands that the needle on the pleasure dial always points to the plus side. Instead he counts himself happy if only it isn't on the minus. Alas, he *should* have questioned that initial premise. Woe that he wasn't thinking more clearly.

Related to the idea of painlessness is the idea of annihilation. One would suppose that no one would cheer for nothingness, but oblivion is more popular than you might think. The theme that happiness lies in annihilation comes in three main variations, though they tend to appear in combinations.

The first variation is *You don't exist anyway.* Something like this idea crops up over and over in human history; the best-known version is found in Buddhism. Strictly speaking, such doctrines don't say you have to annihilate yourself, because they don't think there is any *self* there to annihilate. However, they say that the illusion of being a *self* causes endless trouble, just by making suffering possible. To banish the suffering, you have to banish the illusion.

This is still an odd idea, because if the person suffering the illusion isn't real, then it isn't clear who is being exhorted to banish it.

The second variation is *You exist, but you would be better off if you didn't.* In this view, if you can't bring yourself to commit suicide, then you should make yourself as nearly nothing as you can, perhaps by anesthetizing yourself with narcotics, perhaps by meditating upon emptiness. Try not to feel. Try not to think. "Thinking is but an idle waste of thought, and nought is everything, and everything is nought."[3]

But this way of thinking is also a waste of thought. The person contemplating suicide fancies that if only he no longer exists he will be better off, because then he will no longer suffer. But if he does cease to exist, then how can one speak of how well off he is? There must still be *someone* for that *someone* to better off. Thus the suicidal person is trying to imagine an impossible future self who has ceased to exist, *but exists*. On the other hand, if his future self really does exist, then how can he know whether that future self will better off? Why shouldn't he be worse?

The notion of trying to get as close to nothingness as possible doesn't hold up either. Those who use narcotics don't obliterate their thoughts; they merely replace them with stupid thoughts. Those who meditate on emptiness don't empty their minds; they merely fill them with thoughts of emptiness. Whatever unhappiness may make the thought of nothingness attractive, such choices are likely to make unhappiness worse.

The third variation is *What exists isn't yourself, but a string of selves; you are annihilating yourself all the time.* In this view, each mayfly self in the series replaces the one before, each one calling itself *you* merely because it remembers all the previous ones. Each time you do anything whatsoever, the *you* that did the deed ceases to exist by the very fact of doing it, its place taken by the *you* that the doing of the deed brings into existence. You will be much more comfortable, the argument runs, if you accept these facts gracefully and abandon any thought of continuity. For one thing, you can then dispense with having to take responsibility for your actions, because future selves can't be expected to keep the vows and promises of past ones. For another, you can stop worrying about where your life is going, because there isn't any *your life,* and the *you* that was worrying about it an instant ago has already disappeared. Life is just a series of relationships, projects, or masks, put on and taken off like tee shirts. The links don't form a chain. In spring you're "with" one person, in fall "with" another. In January you're "into" one thing, in February "into" another. On Sunday, you wear one mask, on Monday you wear another.

Ultimately, this way of thinking is just as impossible to sustain as the other two we have considered. For to whom are we speaking when we say that *you* will be more comfortable abandoning the thought of continuity? If *you* wear these masks, then isn't there a *you* who wears them? And if *you* accept this mayfly philosophy, then who has accepted it?

These reasons for rejecting the idea that happiness is mere painlessness or annihilation seem cogent. Yet people do not always accept cogent reasons. Why?

Perhaps one cause is emotional: they suffer a pervading sense of suffering, brokenness, tiredness, and the impermanence of all precious things. Yet that cannot be the whole story, because not everyone who suffers these feelings does reach annihilationist conclusions. I think that to become an annihilationist, a person must also consider his shattered condition natural and inevitable, so that—as the Borg say—resistance is futile.

What if our shattered condition is *not* natural and inevitable? I don't think it is; I think the problem is that our condition is unnatural. There is something wrong with us. The lower powers of our nature rebel against the higher. All too often our emotions and appetites conspire against reason instead of cooperating with it. Our passions say to our minds, "To blazes with you. We're the boss." We can even be irate with ourselves *because* we act reasonably.

Now the person who cultivates the discipline of the virtues is trying, by repeated right choices, to get the appetites, passions, and reason back into harness, with reason the boss. By contrast, the person who falls into despair is usually suffering one of two disorders.

First, he may not be seriously attempting the discipline of the virtues. Perhaps he does not understand what they are, or perhaps he is just not interested. Since he cannot put himself in order, everything seems hopeless to him. Second, he may be attempting these disciplines with all his might and yet hitting a wall. However hard he tries to get past it, he slams into it again and again. His strength is not enough, and he has not the strength to be stronger.

We will discuss the latter disorder later in the book, when we take up the question of whether there are any other means of repairing the human condition. But as to the former disorder, all the generations of man testify that the virtues are indispensable. Barring grave misfortune—which cannot be ruled out—if I have the virtues, I can find a good partner in marriage, I can build a strong family, I can practice sturdy friendships, I can pursue decent work, and I can do many other worthwhile things. Whether things fall utterly into ruin is not wholly within my control, but it is not utterly beyond it, either.

But there is still another difficulty besides these. Sometimes it is called motivated irrationality. I pointed out earlier that each variation on the theme of annihilation is incoherent. It cuts the ground from under its own feet, like the statement "I just *know* that truth cannot be known." Yet some people try to make their peace with having the ground cut out from under them.

I once had a conversation in which the fellow with whom I was speaking committed himself to a literally incoherent position. Gently (I hope), I brought the incoherency to his attention. You might think he would deny it. Instead, he remarked, "I guess I *am* being incoherent." After a moment, he added, "But that's all right, because the universe is incoherent, and I don't need meaning in my life."

A statement like that is a smokescreen. The proper answer is, "I don't believe you. You know as well as I do that the longing for meaning and coherency is deep-set in every mind. So what is it that is so important to you that you are willing to give up even meaning, even coherency, to have it?"

The philosopher Thomas Nagel's famous article, "The Absurd," concludes, "If *sub specie aeternitatis* there is no reason to believe that anything matters, then that doesn't matter either, and we can approach our absurd lives with irony instead of heroism or despair."[4] Some people claim to find the line uplifting. An online reader remarks, "This is the most beautiful thing I've ever read."[5] But if it's true that nothing matters, then what difference does it make whether we live ironically, heroically, or in despair?

Forgive me for being obvious, but if it does make a difference, then something does matter. Our task, should we choose to remain men—and we always have the option of declining—is to find out what.

# CHAPTER 12

# Could Meaning or Commitment Be Happiness?

"It must be a question that burns under their fingernails."[1]

At the end of the last chapter, I claimed that if we say our lives don't need meaning, we delude ourselves. Indeed there is a slice of truth in the notion that happiness lies in meaning itself—at least in something that *has* meaning or involves meaningful commitment, such as challenge or work that seems worthwhile. We are not mindless beasts, but rational beings. A dog can be satisfied by food, mates, and his place in the pack, but relentlessly the human mind seeks to know *what it all means*.

Freud warned of the supposedly dire consequences of sexual repression. Curiously, he didn't say much about the repression of the longing for meaning. The craving for things to mean something leaks, sneaks, or bursts past every attempt to contain it. So strong is it that those who fancy that they believe nothing often seem willing to believe anything.

Though we may be distracted by other desires, the desire for meaning—a thrifty desire that wastes nothing—has its own uses for every one of them. We imagine, for example, that the avaricious man wants nothing but gain, but although some beasts accumulate, the beasts are not interested in gain the way humans are. No animal basks in the thought of how magnificent his pile of stuff makes him, of how great it makes the meaning of Himself. Perhaps the longing for meaning can be bribed or bought off for a while, perhaps the great quest can be delayed, but it cannot be ignored. Most of all we wish to know what our lives mean, what others' lives mean, what it signifies that there is a world and we are in it. Have these desires any point or purpose, or are we like squirrels on an exercise wheel?

The facile and the glib tell us, "Meaning is in the eye of the beholder, things mean whatever you make of them." That would be convenient, wouldn't it? But wait a moment—couldn't these answers be correct? After all, some meanings really are more or less arbitrary; we could have named a little girl Ruby instead of Sapphire, decided that the shape of P would signify the sound of B, or used the word "three" to mean two things and "two" to mean three. And we do "make things" of our lives, for instance by raising a family; sometimes this is called making meaning. But nothing in life means whatever we make of it and nothing more. I may decide to spend my life blowing bubbles or pulling the wings off flies, but no decision of mine can make life *mean* the blowing of bubbles or the pulling of wings off flies. I can't even make one of these two things mean the other one.

Leaving aside the meaning of life as a whole, meaning isn't arbitrary even in the details. A sneering insult means malice; there is no way to make it mean love. A kiss means affection; though it can be used to betray, this deception is possible only because a kiss, in itself, means the opposite of betrayal. (Otherwise, who would submit to being kissed?) Although the meaning of an act can be overwritten by a contradictory meaning, as in the case of the Judas kiss, acts do have underlying meanings. The underlying meaning of an open-faced smile is good will. The underlying meaning of discussion is partnership in a search for understanding. The underlying meaning of marital intercourse is the mutual, total, and exclusive gift of each spouse to the other.

Yes, we can associate anything with anything. Because I once ate a salami sandwich while watching some children at a playground, I may associate childhood with salami. Because a beloved friend was untrue, I may associate friendship with treachery. But even if childhood means salami "to me" or friendship means treachery "to me," the facts remain that the meaning of childhood is not salami, and the meaning of friendship is not treachery.

If anything at all could mean anything at all, we could not even communicate the fact to each other. We could not communicate at all. We might as well run in circles saying, "Ba-ba-ba." Even the despairing statement *Everything is meaningless* can be understood only against the background of a world in which, generally speaking, things do mean things, so that when we can't perceive the meanings that we most long to know we are crushed and tempted to give up.

I don't claim that discerning *what it all means* is easy. Plainly, though, there is a great difference between our "having meaning" and our actually knowing what it all means. Self-concocted meanings are just another variety of distraction, bribe, or payoff, deflecting us from seeking to find out what things mean really. But what does it *mean* to know what it all means? It means knowing *the truth* about what it all means. Meaning in this sense is not something we make up, but something we discover. We may have discovered only pieces of the truth, but in each piece that we think we've got, we have either got it right or got it wrong.

It is amazing how easily we overlook the futility of self-concocted meanings. Consider the philosophers who speak of what they call the "basic good of religion" or the "positive" psychologists who speak of what they call "transcendence." Those are nice words, judging by the sound of them. But as these writers use them, they turn out to signify nothing more than connection or commitment with a source of meaning greater than we are—work, the nation, the revolution, whatever it may be. The source doesn't have to be a true source. It just has to be a source.

What if we choose a false source? In Twelve-Step groups like Alcoholics Anonymous, the Second Step is affirming that "[We] came to believe that a Power greater than ourselves could restore us to sanity."[2] Some years ago I read a newspaper article by a reporter who went around asking the members of Twelve-Step groups what they took this Power to be. They gave all sorts of answers. One told the reporter, "For me, it's electricity."

Perhaps the man who said this identified with the fellow in the old Ray Bradbury tale who thought he was in touch with the All because he drowsed off while listening to the hum of high-tension power lines going everywhere. I'm sorry, the meaning of life is not electricity. Nor is the meaning of life the All, which is only Everything. Yes, my life is one thing amidst the totality of life and death, animals and stars, harmonicas and pneumonia, pop concerts and yogurt smoothies, love, malice, lies, truths, and illusions. But saying that my life is part of *all that* is no good unless I know what all that *means*—and we are back to square one.

Indeed, the All or the Everything is one of the sillier candidates for meaning. The cosmos is not a greater thing than a person, but a lesser one. It has no knowledge, will, or self-awareness. We know it exists; it doesn't know that we exist. We know it is beautiful; it doesn't even know that there is such a thing as beauty. Perhaps it seems greater than we are because we are parts of it, but the statement that we are parts of it is equivocal. My hand is a part of me in the sense that the actions that I perform with my hand are *my own* actions. If you asked me who scrambled the breakfast eggs, I wouldn't say, "The hand attached to me scrambled them," but "I scrambled them, using my hand." I am not part of the cosmos in that sense, but only in the sense that I am inside it, the way I am inside my kitchen. I don't say that the kitchen scrambled the eggs, making use of me. I scrambled them. The kitchen is not the responsible party. I am. I am greater than the kitchen. In the same way, I am greater than the cosmos. So is every other distinct person.

But let us not digress about the All. To further elucidate the fallacy I have been describing, let me return to one of my previous examples, the so-called positive psychologists. They are not interested in whether the meanings we attribute to life are true meanings, but only in whether we attribute meanings to life. Why? Because doing so is one of the things that give us "positive feelings."

For example, psychologist Jonathan Haidt uses such terms as "divinity," "sacredness," and "elevation" for nothing but the feeling of uplift—for feeling *as though* a reality other than our everyday reality has been revealed to us.[3] One might think Haidt is speaking about God and suggesting that such a reality actually can be revealed to us. No, Haidt, who says he is an atheist, is careful never to suggest that we are ever in touch with such a thing. For him, that doesn't matter. "Even atheists have intimations of sacredness," he explains, "particularly when in love or in nature." He adds, "We just don't infer that God caused those feelings."[4]

Whether God caused those feelings rather misses the point. The question is whether *anything* caused them—whether sacredness is not just a feeling, but a reality to which feelings may respond. Haidt speaks of "intimations of sacredness," but an intimation, properly speaking, is a hint, a sign, or an indication that we are in the presence of something. Haidt doesn't mean that. In his view, the feeling of elevation does not point beyond itself. Its value is that we like having it.

He does think that the feeling of elevation has a secondary value: it prompts people to want to be better and to perform good deeds. Ah, but do they actually become better, and do they really perform the good deeds? Disappointedly, he confesses that according to his research, by and large they don't. "Love could be the answer," he writes.[5] But what, for Haidt, is love? Just another positive feeling. So we are going nowhere. This is how teenagers think. Grownups know that love is not a feeling, but a commitment of the will to the true good of another person. To be sure, it is usually accompanied by feelings, but one may have splendid feelings without loving, and one may love even though feelings have run dry.

Haidt even admits that feelings of elevation can be artificially produced. In a moment of bathos, he reveals that he and his students have experimented with various ways of inducing elevation, and that among the methods that work well are "selections from the Oprah Winfrey Show."[6]

Positive psychologists Christopher Peterson and Martin E. P. Seligman think of meaning in much the same sentimental way. "Transcendence," they say, is a trait of character that supports those "positive feelings." But what do they mean by transcendence? "We define it here in the broad sense, as the connection to something higher—the belief that there is meaning or purpose larger than ourselves."[7] Elsewhere Seligman describes how he studies this transcendence: He administers a questionnaire. First he asks subjects to consider whether they have a philosophy of life that tells them their place in the universe, and whether they derive meaning from attachment to something larger than they are. Then he asks them to give themselves scores on two items: Whether they have a calling in life, and whether their lives have strong purpose. "This," he says, "is your spirituality score."[8]

By this measure, those who believed in Hitler would surely have had very high spirituality scores. So would the followers of Stalin, Mao, and Pol Pot, and the militants of Al Qaeda and ISIS. One supposes that all these people had positive feelings about what they were doing. While the positive psychologists do not include hatred among the positive feelings, they do include love. Loaded as these fanatics were with loving devotion to the cause, it seems that the positive psychologists should say that they were happy.

I am not thinking so much of the sheer wickedness of such personalities and movements, as of the fact that their ideologies are false. Can a person whose life is based on a delusion be called happy? Some would say, "Ignorance is bliss." And if bliss is nothing but good feelings, they are right. But we have already considered this idea and found it wanting.

In considering whether a life based on a delusion can be called happy, we might also ponder Solon's contention, examined by Aristotle, that we cannot properly judge whether someone has led a happy life until he has died. He was not merely suggesting that up until the point of death, something may change for the worse (although that is true). The deeper point of his remark is that before someone dies, we cannot see the pattern of his life as a whole.[9]

Let us imagine an attorney and statesman who devotes his career to proving the innocence of a group of persons who have been imprisoned (he thinks falsely) for conspiring in cruel and violent crimes. Admired by his fellows, applauded for his selflessness, he labors in the courts and finally triumphs, for in the final act of his life, the felons are freed. But in the epilogue, while his body is cooling in the ground, we learn that they were guilty after all. Though he didn't live to find out, as soon as they were released they went on a terroristic spree, torturing, raping, and dismembering scores of persons.

Would you say the man's life was a blessed one? Was it fulfilled? Did it attain its end? Most people would say no. The man himself would say no.

A hope truly worth hoping is to discover the meanings that truly inhere in things. By themselves, mere feelings of meaning are but a higher hedonism, and mere beliefs about them, blind guides. They are not only worthless, but perilous. It's true that some of the meanings we attribute to things have more of the smell of the truth, even if they are not, simply, true. They may even be milestones on the path to the real thing—which is not just to *know about* the true meaning of things but to be *taken up into* that meaning, a possibility we will not discuss until much later. Good! But convictions about meaning can also function like vaccines, for unfortunately, worse beliefs about *what it all means* may sometimes inoculate us against better ones.

Anyway, the value of elevated feelings is not that they tickle our pleasure centers, but that they prick the longing for what is higher. Turning our faces skyward, perhaps we will glimpse real and lofty things we would not otherwise have known. Taking to heart what we glimpse there, perhaps we will commit ourselves to what not only seems greater than we are, but is. Everything else is smoke, spray, blood, spume, and vanity.

# CHAPTER 13

## Could Love or Friendship Be Happiness?

"Well did one say to his friend: Thou half of my soul."[1]

According to one common view, friends are wonderful, "love is all you need," and if only you have friends and love you will live happily ever after. This sets an awfully high bar for relationships, and legions of disappointed people lurch to the opposite extreme. In their view, friendship is a weak reed, love is unreliable, and you can't ever trust yourself to another person.

Although views about ordinary friendship swing between the same two extremes, the contrast is probably most vivid in erotic relationships. Typical expressions of the love-is-all-you-need view range the gamut from fairytale princesses who live happily ever after to the steamy pulp novels mislabeled "romances" these days. Typical of the never-trust-anyone view was the remark of a young woman who attended a talk about marriage I gave at a liberal arts college. I had argued that matrimonial love asks the husband and wife to give themselves totally, exclusively, and mutually to each other. She spoke up during the Q&A to say, "If that's what marriage really is, you're pushing me away from it more and more." No gift of self for her; she owned herself utterly—and intended to go on doing so. In her view, apparently, marriage was but an arrangement of convenience between two parties who make each other's acquaintance but who never quite meet.

Some people oscillate between these two extremes. Some try to have it both ways. So what if friendship is unreliable? Drench yourself in the feelings while they last! Get hurt over and over! That's life!

Why do we stagger between cheerful, rosy naïveté and bleak, selfish cynicism? What is so wonderful about love and friendship, and what is so disheartening about them? Let us first consider what these words might mean. According to a very old suggestion, friendship comes in three kinds. One sort is based on pleasure and commiseration. Most friendships among the young are of this kind; they have fun together, and perhaps weep together. The second sort of friendship is based on mutual usefulness. This kind is found especially among persons in business and politics; they make deals and exchange favors. But the truest sort of friendship, the one most deserving of the name, the reality of which those other two are but shadows, is a partnership in a good life, bound by a commitment of the will. I will my friend's good. I will my friend's good *for* my friend. I will it not as something alien to me, but as my *own* good. The name of this commitment is love.

It is a little risky using this term, because in English the word "love" is used for so many things. To many people today the word means sex, and it is true that the intensity of the marital friendship can reach great heights. But there are many kinds of friendship, and a certain kind of love is native to each. The friendship of brothers, the friendship of colleagues, the friendship of companions in a task—in themselves, these and many other kinds of love lack the least trace of eros. The converse is also true: there are many erotic relationships that lack the least trace of love or friendship.

In some cultures friends speak freely of their feelings. In others they are reticent. Although Americans have little reticence in general, men in our sex-obsessed society rarely speak of what their friendships with other men mean to them, for fear that these admissions might be taken in a sexual light. Yet the intensity of nonsexual friendship can rival the intensity of eros, and in cultures that unambiguously repudiate sex between men, there is no need to fear misunderstanding. Thus the biblical David, writing in tribute of his slain friend Jonathan, exclaims, "I grieve for you, Jonathan my brother! Most dear have you been to me; more precious have I held love for you than love for women."[2]

Setting sexual passion aside, the emotions associated with love in general arise from the good things the friends accomplish together—in the case of spouses, for example, raising their family, and in the case of fellow strugglers in a cause, mutual commitment and help. These emotions include *confidence* that what they have begun well will get better, *exultation* because each glories in the other's good, *consolation* because their delight in a shared good gives each a remedy against sadness, and a certain *exuberance* because their work together lifts low spirits and overcomes even grave tribulation.[3]

But these emotions are not themselves love. They spring up because friends, with all their hearts, concur in something good apart from feelings. For if I love you, then not only am I glad of your existence, but I also seek your good, and I know it is good that I do so. I want you to be, I want you to live, I want good things *for* you, I want to *do* good things for you, I even want to do good things *because* of you. Good itself seems better because of you.

This view of love, as a commitment of the will, is most spectacularly on display in the Western marriage vows, because the spouses *promise* to love. Even more pointedly, they promise to go on loving even if things work out badly: "For better or for worse." If love really was a feeling, then such a promise would be impossible because although, as we have seen, we have more influence over our feelings than we like to admit, this influence is not complete, and feelings fluctuate. But my will is something I direct. I can bind my will to pursue your true good. I can settle myself to learn the practices and disciplines that such a will entails. I can determine upon this will even if our friendship is strained—even if at this minute I find it difficult to see eye to eye with you, or even to enjoy your company. And if I do this, perhaps even my feelings will come back around.

Love is costly. It makes me spend myself, even makes me *want* to spend myself. But there is something strange about this spending, because in the perfection of love my friend is "another self."[4] Even though I forget myself, I am not diminished by the forgetting. I lose myself, only to find myself in a more spacious continent. But no such discovery is possible if the will is unwilling to be bound.

Love has the fragrance of eternity, yet for finite beings it also has a scent of fear, of precariousness, of risk of loss. Why? One reason is that since my happiness is now joined with the happiness of someone else, I am vulnerable. Another is that although will is a stronger thing than feelings, the will is not made of dead stuff like lead or stone; one might say that our will is made of us. Hence the friends could ruin their love; they could lose it; they could lose each other forever. Though "love is strong as death,"[5] what we imagine to be love often suffers death. I lose much more if I never risk loss; yet the risk is real.

And how often are even lovers tempted to use, devour, or take advantage of each other instead of giving themselves to each other! And though I have written "even lovers," couldn't I have written "especially lovers"? Abundance of passion is no remedy for the problem. No wonder many mortals give up on love completely! How many others, though giving in to the longing for some kind of love, set their sights as low as possible! At times it may seem that the communion of two beings does nothing but open new possibilities to cause each other sorrow. Ah, my dear, if I didn't love you, you couldn't hurt me as much as you do. If you didn't love me, the wound I give your heart wouldn't sting so dreadfully like death.

It may be said that this imperfection of mortal friendship, the fact that we do not love well enough and may let each other down, has a cure because it is a disease: let us love each other better. May we implement this cure! But mortal friendship faces another problem besides its imperfection—its *insufficiency*, which cannot be cured, because, unlike the imperfection of love, it is not a disease. What I mean is that even when we do love well, mortal love is not enough. Not because we love so poorly, but *in itself and by its essence*, love is not enough. For all its beauty, precisely because of its beauty, it cannot satisfy us completely—and the more deeply someone loves, the more keenly he feels this to be true.

This is especially, agonizingly true in erotic love. Nothing so fully promises completeness, nothing so intensifies the longing for it as the teasing foretaste of it in bodily union. Yet so great is the yearning aroused by this foretaste that nothing falls so short! No two people can be everything to each other for long.

Some people take this point too literally. They think that since no *two* people can be everything to each other, the problem of insufficiency can be overcome by adding a few more people—whether by way of polygamy, polyamory, so-called open marriage, or outright cheating. This is a delusion, for it makes the insufficiency infinitely worse. In erotic love I not only want to give, I want to give my very self. But I cannot divide myself into parts; the only way to give myself at all is to give myself completely and exclusively. If I say, "I give twenty-five percent of myself to each of you," I am not really giving myself to anyone. Aren't love poems all over the world addressed from the lover to the beloved? A lyric "to my darlings, Mary, Ellen, Susan,

Penelope, Martha, Hortense, and Gwen" would be recognized every-where as farce.

The insufficiency of mortal love is a fact that even the most devoted lovers eventually confront. Many are those who would rather not love than endure love's malaise and deficiency—many who would rather give up that fragrance of eternity, just because it is only a fragrance. So even if the human lover gives himself, somehow not even all of him is enough. The beloved cries to the mortal lover, "Why, after wounding this heart, have you not healed it?" because no mortal can heal it.

What is the root of this wound? I think it lies in the fact that the lovers' desire for the beloved both ignites and obscures a second, different desire—one that they may not have expected and may not even recognize—one we will meet again later in the book. Their erotic longing provokes a mysterious second longing, of which eros, by itself, is only an image. Because this strange second longing is not eros, but is only awakened by eros, it cannot be appeased by eros. This is why the Shulammite adjures her sisters who are not yet wounded, "that you stir not up nor awaken love until it please."[6]

And yet, O happy chance! she is not sorry for her wound. It is not one that kills, but one that gives life. She would rather suffer the wound without healing than never have been pierced in the first place; she would rather yearn without fulfillment than never have been awakened to the yearning.

Confusion of the two longings—of erotic longing per se with the other longing that erotic longing awakens—brings many lovers to grief. They expect their embraces to satisfy not only the longing that embraces can satisfy, but also the longing that embraces stir up and cannot satisfy. Demanding that their love satisfy the second longing too, they become tyrannical. Discovering that it cannot be satisfied, they misdiagnose the problem. He thinks, *It is my wife's fault.* She thinks, *It is my husband's fault.* They think, *It is the fault of our marriage.* Or perhaps they blame faithfulness, promises, or love itself.

There is nothing wrong with faithfulness, promises, or love. There may not even be anything wrong with these particular husbands, wives, or marriages. What vexes these souls is that they are getting the first, appeasable longing mixed up with the second, unappeasable longing.

Suppose we could have the appeasable longing without the unappeasable one—suppose we could experience eros without the transcendent something that it so terribly resembles. Would that be better? No, because that transcendent something is the very thing that makes eros what it is for human beings. Without it, passion would be nothing more than sex, as it is among the animals—a bodily stress, followed by relief, perhaps with an added urge to nest.

Who knows? Together, the lovers might seek to find out whether anything really can appease that second longing. Together, they may find greater success than either could have found by hunting for the answer alone. That is an aspiration truly worthy of their love.

But perfect happiness cannot lie in any form of mortal love, because the lovers are not the remedy for this sweet wound; they are but the balm that makes the sweet wound endurable.

CHAPTER 14

## Could Virtue Be Happiness?

"Know then this truth (enough for man to know),
Virtue alone is happiness below."[1]

O ur discussion so far has given us good reason to think that
without virtue, other goods are scarcely good. Could virtue
itself, then, be happiness?

Dozens of thinkers have sworn that it is. Seneca asked, "Pray tell
me what return one gets for righteousness, innocence, magnanimity,
chastity, temperance? If you wish for anything beyond these virtues,
you do not wish for the virtues themselves."[2] Nearer our time, Spinoza declared, "Blessedness is not the reward of virtue, but virtue
itself."[3] The motto, "Virtue is its own reward" is a cultural common-
place.

Probably few of those who say such things mean them in the
literal sense. Rather than thinking that virtue alone will bring happiness, they may think merely that though virtue is the noblest good,
other things too are sweet, and virtue alone is insufficient. Even so,
the unadulterated idea has had plenty of defenders, the first and most
famous of them Socrates:

*Polus*: What! and does all happiness consist in this?
*Socrates*: Yes, indeed, Polus, that is my doctrine; the men
and women who are gentle and good are also happy, as I
maintain, and the unjust and evil are miserable.[4]

In the same vein, Marcus Tullius Cicero exults, "If then it is happiness to rejoice in such goods of the soul, that is, virtues...we are bound to admit that they are all happy." Brutus asks, "Even in torture and upon the rack?" Cicero fires back, "Do you think I meant on beds of violets and roses?"[5] Elsewhere he says, "You do not know, foolish man, you do not know what power virtue possesses; you only usurp the name of virtue; you are a stranger to her influence. No man who is wholly consistent within himself, and who reposes all his interests in himself alone, can be other than completely happy."[6]

But much earlier, Aristotle had dismissed this idea. "Those who say that the victim on the rack or the man who falls into great misfortunes is happy if he is good, are, whether they mean to or not, talking nonsense."[7] This seems so obvious that many readers will be content to end the chapter here. Sometimes, though, there may be reasons to change our minds even about things we think plain. A theory is best tested at its highest point, and those who made the highest effort to prove the sufficiency of virtue were the Stoics. So before passing on, let's consider whether even the Stoics could make the theory that virtue is happiness work.

For clarity: In speaking of virtue, we don't mean just doing right things, but having right traits of character; a thief is not praised for honesty if he abstains from theft while being watched. Nor are we asking whether we should practice virtue even if it doesn't make us happy, but whether virtue *is itself* happiness.[8] We aren't asking whether the truly virtuous can bear sorrow, but whether they are free of it.

The nobility of Stoicism comes from its insistence on the point we aren't investigating—that we should always practice virtue. But the strained quality of its arguments comes from its insistence that happiness lies in virtue and nothing else. How is it even possible to suppose that the Sage who practices virtue is happy when his bones are pulled from their sockets, his body shudders in poverty, or he is exiled from friends and family?

The Stoic answer: happiness is in the mind alone, and circumstances like torture, poverty, and exile are outside it. We are always free to decide what to make of such "externals," because the virtuous mind is sovereign within its domain. Marcus Aurelius consoles himself, "if you remove the opinion 'I have been harmed,' then you remove the complaint; if you remove the complaint, then you remove the harm." Why? Because "if something outside you gives pain, what disturbs you is not the thing but your judgment about it. It is in your power to wipe out this judgment now."⁹

With apologies to John Donne, the attitude of the Stoic sage is that he *is* an island, entire of itself. Though he makes brave talk about being but a part of the cosmos, in fact he thinks he is sovereign, set apart from the rest of its inhabitants. Cicero describes the Stoic wise man as one who is "wholly consistent within himself, and who reposes all his interests in himself alone"¹⁰—and he considers this good. Epictetus goes so far as to say that refusing to view anything as harmful makes us independent not only of enemies but of friends. "Do we not remember that no man either hurts another or does good to another, but that a man's opinion about each thing is that which hurts him, is that which overturns him…?"¹¹ We may be forgiven for thinking that this kind of virtue is more like a vice—or perhaps two vices, selfishness and pride.

According to Epictetus, the fortress of the Stoic soul is impregnable. Sound doctrine declares, "Men, if you will attend to me, wherever you are, whatever you are doing, you will not feel sorrow, nor anger, nor compulsion, nor hindrance, but you will pass your time without perturbations and free from everything." A man who has this peace rightly reflects, "Now no evil can happen to me; for me there is no robber, no earthquake, everything is full of peace, full of tranquillity: every way, every city, every meeting, neighbor, companion is harmless."[12]

Cicero agrees: "For surely virtue gives sufficient to make us live bravely; if bravely, sufficient too to make us high-souled and in fact never appalled by any event and always undefeated. It follows that there is no repentance, no deficiency, no obstacle: There is then always abundance, perfection, prosperity, therefore happiness.... For just as folly... never thinks it has obtained enough; so wisdom is always contented with its present lot and is never self-repentant."[13]

Yet sometimes even Cicero finds Stoicism hard to stomach. For although the Stoics claim that virtue is the sole good and all other things are indifferent, they also say that the virtuous man seeks some of these indifferent things and avoids others. Papering over the inconsistency, they declare that some indifferent things are "preferred." As Cicero protests, "How can you have a greater inconsistency than for the same person to say both that [virtue] is the sole good and that we have a natural instinct to seek the things conducive to life?"[14] He challenges anyone who would speak that way: "Let him prove that I shall be readier to despise money if I believe it to be a 'thing preferred' than if I believe it to be a good, and braver to endure pain if I say it is irksome and hard to bear and contrary to nature, than if I call it an evil."[15]

The most convincing testimony that the Stoics could not really live out their doctrine was their defense of suicide. Chrysippus enumerated various justifications for doing away with oneself, such as escaping poverty or illness.[16] Other Stoics compare suicide with leaving a room:

- "Has it smoked in the chamber? If the smoke is moderate, I will stay; if it is excessive, I go out: for you must always remember this and hold it fast, that the door is open."[17]
- "Remember this: the door is open; be not more timid than little children, but as they say, when the thing does not please them, 'I will play no longer,' so do you, when things seem to you of such a kind, say I will no longer play, and begone: but if you stay, do not complain."[18]
- "The greatest boon with which grudging Nature has equipped man is this—that the door of death stands open and suffers us to depart from a life that is too hard."[19]

Some fans of Stoicism—and as the great oracle Twitter discloses, there are more of those than you might think—consider the doctrine of suicide cheering. Augustine saw that it is closer to despair:

> I am at a loss to understand how the Stoic philosophers can presume to say that these are no ills, though at the same time they allow the wise man to commit suicide and pass out of this life if they become so grievous that he cannot or ought not to endure them.... O happy life, which seeks the aid of death to end it! If it is happy, let the wise man remain in it; but if these ills drive him out of it, in what sense is it happy?[20]

If courage is the virtue that measures all the other ones in the showdown, then what are we to make of the Stoic who does cut his wrists, saying like a pouty child, "I won't play any more"? Part of his problem is that he misunderstands the relationship between virtue and emotion. Yes, the passions need guidance from reason—but as I have suggested, the mark of reason's guidance isn't having no feelings, but feeling the right things, at the right times, about the right objects, towards the right people, with the right motive, and in the right way.[21] We would be just as wretched having no emotions as being yanked around by them. For example, when the mind says, "Here is evil," properly regulated anger assists by arousing us to the defense of endangered goods, and properly regulated fear assists by arousing us to retreat from evils that cannot be overcome.

But the Stoics considered desires and emotions "infections." Instead of viewing virtue as governing these fluctuating things, they thought that it annihilated them. Rather than the ordinary desires and emotions, they wanted to experience what they called "constant states"—the constant state of "will" would replace desire, the constant state of "contentment" would replace joy, and the constant state of "caution" would replace fear. The condition that they aspired to they called *apatheia*, "apathy," which meant something like untouchability. "No fears alarm, no distresses corrode, no lusts inflame, no vain transports of delight dissolve in the melting lassitude of pleasure. . . . And if virtue makes this possible, what reason is there why virtue of its own power alone should not make men happy?"[22]

As the ever-mordant Jonathan Swift remarked, "The Stoical scheme of supplying our wants by lopping off our desires is like cutting off our feet when we want shoes."[23] I think Swift was generous.

Can we really lop off our desires, anyway? Persons striving along the Stoic path found that they were just as exposed to the turbulence of desires as others were. Their teachers said this was because nothing less than *perfect* virtue is of any use at all. They promised that although all along the way the sojourner will suffer, all in a flash he will experience a Change or Conversion[24] and become tranquil. Just as a drowning man is unable to breath whether he is five hundred fathoms or one cubit from the surface, they said, so a man is lost to happiness whether he is a long way from virtue or getting close. Just as the blind cannot see even if they are going to regain their sight, so those advancing toward virtue are stupid and depraved until they get there.[25] But when they *do* get there, they can see and they can breathe.

From the fact that they offered such vivid illustrations, wouldn't you think that the Stoics had experienced this Conversion? Alas, they had not. Seneca turns what should have been a humble confession into a sullen boast: "I am not wise, and, just to nourish your ill will: *I will not be wise.* Demand from me, then, not that I am equal to the best but that I am better than the bad. It is enough for me to subtract something from my vices each day and to chastise my own mistakes. I have not arrived at good health, *nor will I indeed arrive.* I am concocting balms rather than cures for my 'gout,' content if it visits me less often and less acutely. Yet compared with your feet, you weaklings, I am a runner" [emphasis added].[26]

It seems that the Stoics' wise man, who needs nothing but his virtue for his happiness, does not exist. And if not even the Stoics could consistently uphold the view that virtue is happiness, I think we may conclude that no one could. We already knew that true virtue contributes enormously to happiness, but we would have to tie our minds behind our backs to think that no more is needed.

# CHAPTER 15

## Does It All Come Down to Luck?

"Don't put it all on the line for just one roll.
You've got to have an ace in the hole."[1]

A plausible response to the conclusions of the previous chapter is to say that although virtue alone is not enough for happiness, happiness lies in good character *plus good fortune*—in virtue plus "everything else." Of course it would be impossible to list literally everything in "everything else." All sorts of things that we haven't yet discussed might be included, such as having enough variety in life not to get bored. Presumably good fortune would be having the right amount or degree of everything—whatever that is.

We will return to the possibility that happiness lies in virtue plus good fortune in the next chapter. For now let's ask a different question: Could it be that happiness lies in good fortune alone? Could it be at least that luck overshadows all the other contributions to happiness?

The most venerable retort is that even though luckless good people do suffer, still luck is less important to happiness than virtue. But the spokesmen for Lady Fortune have an answer to that: whether we gain virtue is also just luck!

Before we consider these claims and counterclaims, suppose luck really were the supreme arbiter of happiness. How, in that case, should we live? It would be senseless to make plans, lay up firewood against a cold day, or try to become a certain kind of person. Let life happen as it may! But hold on. In that case, whether one were the kind of person who makes plans or who lets everything happen as it may would also be in the luck of the draw.

Cicero thought that if luck were truly sovereign we would have nothing left to do but pray.[2] Many nations do put a goddess of luck in their pantheons. Gamblers murmur invocations to her. An old Broadway favorite complains, "They call you Lady Luck, but there is room for doubt; at times you have a very un-ladylike way of running out."[3] Machiavelli—how seriously, we don't know—spoke of her as a fickle woman who tends to give her favors, such as they are, to audacious young men who treat her roughly.[4]

But if everything depended on luck, then wouldn't the goddess's favors depend on luck too? It would make no more sense to pray hard than to work hard.

Does anyone *really* think luck omnipotent? As Plutarch wrote, "Nobody wets clay with water and leaves it, assuming that by chance and accidentally there will be bricks, nor after providing himself with wool and leather does he sit down with a prayer to Chance that they turn into a cloak and shoes for him."[5] Yet even if they don't quite believe it, people often speak as though good and bad fortune did rule everything. Why?

Let's make a distinction. There are motives for speaking this way, and then there are reasons.

The motives are various, including consolation ("since it's all luck, there's no point in worrying how things will turn out"), pity ("it's not his fault he never got the breaks), complaint ("why doesn't life ever give *me* a break?"), extenuation ("things always go wrong for me, but that's just my luck"), and envy ("you only have more because you're lucky, so hand over some of it to me").

The reasons, as distinct from the motives, seem to be twofold. One of them is careless generalization. Since some things depend at least *partly* on luck, it may seem that all of them, or at least the most important, depend *entirely* on luck. You come from a respectable family; I'm from the wrong side of the tracks. You've got good health; I've got bad eyes, bad feet, and bad lungs. Your voice induces respect; my accent makes people laugh. I was caught in the layoff. My side lost the war. I'm dying.

In a dark enough mood, even the bravest person may curse the power of fortune. "For my part," says Cicero to his Stoic friend, "when I consider with myself the hazards in which fortune has tried me so severely, there are moments when I begin to lose confidence in this opinion of yours and feel exceeding fear of the weakness and frailty of mankind. For I am afraid that nature in giving us, to begin with, feeble bodies, with which she has combined both incurable diseases and unendurable pains, has also given us souls that both share in the suffering of physical pain and, apart from this, have their own entanglement of trouble and vexation."[6]

Moreover, the power of wisdom and foresight to head off calamities is limited. It's true that a person of practical wisdom considers his situation carefully, anticipates the things that may happen, and plans accordingly. Yet as Swift pointed out, the least slip or accident may change things so radically that "at last he is just as much in doubt of events as the most ignorant and inexperienced person."[7]

This fact leads us to the second reason for overestimating luck, which might be called statistical. Some people doubt whether there even is such a thing as practical wisdom, and they rest their case on the calculation of odds.

Suppose that each of us has to make ten important decisions over the course of a life, but that we really don't know what we are doing, so we might as well be tossing coins. If the chance of each decision coming out well is 50–50, then for most people some decisions will come out well and some won't. Yet in a sufficiently large group, there will be a small number—about 1 out of every 1,024—for whom all ten come out well.[8] Everyone will think these people are very wise, when in fact they're just very lucky.

This argument devastated me when I was a young man, encountering it as a student in a graduate seminar. It shouldn't have, because it assumes what it is trying to prove. True, in a large enough group of people, a few will make all the right decisions even if only by chance. But it doesn't follow that they *did* make them all by chance. We may be confusing the chance that someone without prudence will make the right choices with the chance that someone does have prudence and so makes the right choices because of it. Though the flattering mantra "There is no such thing as a good or bad decision" is widespread in pop culture (if you don't believe me, try googling it), the difference between good and bad decisions is often pretty obvious. "I won't snort cocaine, because it can induce panic, paranoia, seizures, strokes, coma, cardiac arrest, and violent outbreaks." Good decision. "I will snort cocaine, because I like the feeling." Bad one.

There are also motives and reasons for *denying* that happiness is all luck. One motive is self-encouragement: if I refuse to bow down before fortune, then I will never give up. A darker one is self-congratulation: as Swift sardonically remarks, the miserable confess the power of fortune, but those who are doing well attribute all their success to their merits.[9]

But motives aside, the best *reason* to deny the omnipotence of luck is that even granting Swift's point, good character helps us play the hand luck deals us. Plutarch said of Alexander the Great, "even though he became great through fortune, he is even greater in that he made good use of his fortune. And the more we praise his fortune the more shall we exalt his virtue by reason of which he became worthy of his fortune."[10] We don't have to approve Plutarch's judgment of the virtue of Alexander (I don't) to approve the principle. Thrift assists me when I don't have much money. Fortitude helps me cope with losses and fight against ills. Patience enables me to wait for better times. And why should I believe better times will never come? "A fire has opened the way to flight. Men have been let down softly by a catastrophe. Sometimes the sword has been checked even at the victim's throat. Men have survived their own executioners. Even bad fortune is fickle. Perhaps it will come, perhaps not; in the meantime it is not."[11]

Moreover, the coin of good and evil fortune is double-sided. Granted, to a starving man it would be cold consolation to recite Shakespeare's lines about the sweetness of the uses of adversity.[12] Better to give him food. Yet what man or woman has not learned more from sorrow than from complacency and comfort? The obverse is that good things are not always good *for us*. One writer has even suggested that "we need greater virtues to sustain good than evil fortune."[13] Why? Just because the better things go, the more things can go wrong? No, there is more: Aristotle remarked that "even good fortune itself when in excess is an impediment, and perhaps should then be no longer called good fortune."[14]

Ruin lies not just in having too much, but in making bad use of the excess. Consider just a few of the goods we have discussed in this book. Wealth for our needs is good, but wealth beyond them brings sloth, false confidence, and anxiety. A pleasing appearance is good, but beauty exposes us to vanity, unwanted attention, and the suspicion that we owe our positions to looks alone. A decent self-respect is good, but thinking too much or too highly of ourselves is a sucking swamp of illusion. Meaning and commitment are good, but false meanings are idols, and misguided commitments deceivers. Finally, although virtue is indispensable, the imperfect shadow of it can twist our lives into knots. For what if I am brave about the wrong things? And anyway, whose virtue is perfect?

But wait: Couldn't virtue itself depend on luck? Certainly some traits of character are influenced by chance. Everyone who has raised children knows that they are not (thank God) mere putty in their parents' hands. One baby is whiny and fussy, another cheerful; one serious, another hilarious; one stubborn, another easy-going. These native temperaments that so greatly affect the human chances of happiness are present from the moment of birth. Of course parents have great influence on their children, but the children's temperaments limit what they can do.

Now unlike native temperaments, the virtues are acquired. Yet our prospects for their acquisition may also depend partly on luck. If my parents are sullen, I am more likely to grow up sullen; if patient, patient; if greedy, greedy. If they pass on to me a genetic predisposition for alcoholism, I am more likely to have trouble with drink, and if for a tendency to rage, I am more likely to blow up when annoyed. "To one is given ten, to another five."[15] I can't choose my parents or genes. They too are in the luck of the draw.

On the other hand, even though genetics and upbringing influence the acquisition of virtue, they are not virtue themselves. For example, I may have a predisposition to make light of danger, but the virtue of courage requires knowing *when* to take risks. Besides, thinking the predispositions we get from genetics and upbringing determine everything would be as foolish as thinking that they have no weight at all. We do have some control over our moods and states of mind, and we can learn to have more of it; in fact this is largely what virtue is about.

For suppose my personality is morose. Am I doomed to eternal disgruntlement? If I always give in to my sulks, yes—but not if I keep them on a tight leash. Suppose I anger easily. Am I fated to lead a violent life? No—though I will have to work harder than other people to curb my temper. The timid person can resist his fear and learn spunk; the reckless one can restrain his heedlessness and learn caution. "Wisdom has built her house, she has set up her seven pillars. She has slaughtered her beasts, she has mixed her wine, she has also set her table. She has sent out her maids to call from the highest places in the town, 'Whoever is simple, let him turn in here!'"[16]

One might wish that the researches of psychologists would shed light on all this. Unfortunately, the false alternative "nature vs. nurture" takes free will off the table. Have researchers shown that there is no such thing as free will? No, they merely assume it out of existence because they don't know how to fit it into a causal analysis. Ironically, they take their own freedom for granted. For if 100 percent of what we do and think really were determined by the combined influence of genetics and environment, then their opinions about the matter would also be determined—and who among them believes that?[17] Don't they believe themselves free to follow the evidence where it leads?

The conclusion? Many of the goods of life—including even the native quirks of personality that hinder or assist us toward virtue—are due partly to luck, and some people do have advantages in life. Sometimes big ones. But in the first place, what we make of these advantages is due to good choices, not luck, and though good fortune may give us certain tendencies, it does not have the power to give or withhold virtue itself. And in the second place, fortune is deceptive. What we call good luck may sometimes work to our ruin; what we call bad luck may hold lessons that good luck cannot teach. And so whoever scorns fortune's influence is naïve—but whoever bows down to it is a fool.

# CHAPTER 16

# Could Anything in This World Be Happiness?

"Whoever drinks of this water will thirst again."[1]

S uppose, then, that we have both virtue and luck, that charmed combination of good character and unbroken good fortune. Then will all desire be lulled? Will we be fulfilled at last?

No.

Although, as always, I appeal to common knowledge, permit me to use myself to illustrate a point about the lulling of all desire. In the midst of certain experiences there comes over me a certain longing. It is a desire for a Far Something that neither fortune nor character can provide. Often it stirs when I gaze into the face of the moon and starry sky; sometimes, when I look, really look, upon the face of another person. I see, in retrospect, that I have experienced this longing since childhood, but I was not sufficiently reflective to be aware of it until my early teens. The desire is not constant in strength, and at times I can almost forget it. Yet it is profound and compelling.

Not everyone talks about this sort of thing, but probably most people have experienced it, whether while contemplating the celestial courts, like me—or, say, while walking in a forest, hearing the call of a mourning dove, watching the intricate beauty of a dance, grasping a mathematical truth, or seeing the world reflected in a mirror. Whittaker Chambers seems to have experienced it upon gazing at the convolutions of his newborn baby's ear.[2] C.S. Lewis speaks of "that unnameable something, desire for which pierces us like a rapier at the smell of a bonfire, the sound of wild ducks flying overhead, the title of *The Well at the World's End*, the opening lines of *Kubla Khan*, the morning cobwebs in late summer, or the noise of falling waves."[3] Elsewhere he tells how upon reading the first lines of a poem by Henry Wadsworth Longfellow, he "desired with almost sickening intensity something never to be described."[4] Longfellow himself describes it as "a feeling of sadness and longing that is not akin to pain."[5]

Now longing, like certain other passions, is directional. Just as my anger is *at someone*, my longing is *for something*. So what is this longing for? To what is it trying to compel me?

Since it so often comes while I am gazing at the moon, is it a desire for the moon? Surely not. If title to the earth's satellite could be signed over to me and I could keep the moon in my garage, the longing would not be satisfied. It would only attach itself to something else, which would be easy enough, since other things arouse it too. So when I experience this longing, what is it that I want? Various suggestions might be offered.

*What you want is to experience the moon's beauty.* This most obvious suggestion can't be right, because whenever I gaze at the moon I am already beholding its beauty. If what I wanted was to behold it, then I would be satisfied. Yet so far is the experience of its beauty from satisfying my mysterious longing that it even rakes it up. When I go back into my house, sated with the moon's loveliness, the longing is not lulled but still pierces me. By some accident of personality it is associated in my case with the sight of the moon, and

I understand why a pagan might have worshipped the lunar virgin. But it is not a desire to see her beauty.

*What you want is to go there.* I believed this when I was a boy, devouring stories of outer space and travel to the stars. I have no doubt that setting foot on our silver sister would produce a sense of accomplishment and a temporarily exultation. But would it fulfill the longing that I felt and still feel in looking up at the moon? I doubt it. Perhaps you have experienced the strange tang of this longing when looking at the crest of a far-distant hill. Yet when you climbed and attained it, did your conquest of the summit provide what you expected? Getting to the crest satisfies the desire to attain the crest, but it does not satisfy the other desire that is somehow mixed up with it. Stranger yet, you might have experienced that other desire looking *down* again from the crest toward the plain from which you began; and yet it was not satisfied earlier, when you were standing on the plain! In the same way, when I was a boy the longing aroused by the sight of the moon became associated in my mind with the desire to go there, but it was not the same desire. Could I have gone to the moon every day, the desire to go would have been lulled, but my mysterious longing would not have been; it would merely have found new occasions, raising its lance from its secret couch to pierce my heart over again.

*What you want is the sublime and the unattainable as such.* There is a difference between wanting something unattainable, and wanting something *because* it is unattainable. I may want a hamburger and be unable to have one at the moment because I don't have any money. Yet I want the hamburger because I am hungry, not because it is unattainable. Someone might think that the case is different when I gaze at the moon—that its unattainability is the very reason for its charm, and that this is why attaining it would be anticlimactic. Now there is something to this theory. Sometimes low-hanging fruit really is less appealing. Among other things, this is the whole basis of the romantic strategy of playing hard to get. Yet what does it really explain? A prize that more difficult to attain may be more attractive to pursuit than an easy one, but to want something is to want to have it, and to pursue something is to want to catch it. Who in his right mind would tell a thirsty man how lucky he was that whenever he reached for a drink the water was withdrawn? If I do attain the object of pursuit but it leaves me unsatisfied, the proper conclusion is that what I really wanted—or at least the strange something that I *also* wanted—was something else.

*What you want is to be united with the All.* I am happy to be in a universe with snails, tomatoes, garlic, thunderstorms, and galaxies, but who would wish to be united with the aggregate of all these things? To suppose myself united with the aggregate, even if it is an interesting aggregate, is to suppose myself annihilated. Having been annihilated, I could hardly be satisfied in my longing, because I would not *be* at all.

*You are merely experiencing the sublimation of your longing for a woman.* People who have read too much Freud think every mysterious longing is a disguise for libido. Considering the age at which I became aware of the mysterious longing, in my case the suspicion might seem all too plausible. Yet if it were merely sublimated *eros,* then I should no longer feel it when I cast my eye on the moon today. Having been married for a half century to the bride of my youth, I have experienced the satisfaction of *eros,* and love is sweet, but there is this about amorous embraces: they quench only amorous desire. They do not quench the unknown desire that is associated with it. In fact they provide it with new occasions, because the power of the moon's face to arouse it is now rivalled and outdone by the power of the face of the beloved. Lovers will tell you that sometimes the countenance of the one whom they love seems illuminated. Thinking that this glow is just the blush of health or the pink of erotic response, cosmetics vendors offer to counterfeit it with creams and powders. Yet they miss the point, because the light that we see in the face of the beloved is borrowed from Somewhere Else; the face is its mirror and receptacle.

*You are merely experiencing a genetically programmed response to the sight of faraway things and open spaces.* So-called evolutionary psychologists try to explain our sense of beauty in terms of adaptive fitness. As they would have it, since our remote ancestors evolved on the savannah, of course we like distant vistas, such as mountains, moons, horizons, clouds, and seas. Any would-be ancestor that didn't like such prospects would have had difficulty adjusting to his surroundings, and so would have been less likely to pass on his genes—including the gene for liking them. This hypothesis explains nothing. For even if there were an adaptive advantage in liking distant vistas, the fact remains that when I gaze at the moon, I don't just like it, I want something. An unappeasable ache moves in me, a plangent plucking of the strings, not a pain, and yet more like a pain than a pleasure. What could be the adaptive value of having that? Besides, although the moon is my chosen example, human history testifies that the coals of this ache can be raked up and blown into flame by all sorts of things. I don't know what these things might be for you. In my case, another of the things that rakes it up is the very specific experience of hearing Johann Sebastian Bach's *Air on the String of G*. Tell me how that helps me pass on my genes to my progeny.

*You want to experience not just something beautiful, but the ideal of beauty that lies beyond beautiful things.* Here I think we come closer to the truth, though it depends on the meaning of "ideal." This answer is unfashionable in our day. Now there is no need to deny that there are individual differences in the judgment of beauty—I may say the moon is most beautiful, you may confer the honor on the setting sun. Nor is there any need to deny that some kinds of disagreements are more difficult to settle than others—we tend to argue much more about beauty than about, say, weight. But to one degree or another, *all* judgments suffer these difficulties, and they are not good reasons to deny the reality of the things that are judged. The test of any judgment, about anything whatsoever, is whether better reasons can be given for it than for alternative judgments. Suppose someone says that in order to settle a disagreement about which of two rocks is heavier, we need only put them both on a scale, and "That settles it!" Philosophers call this view "naïve empiricism." Why is it called naïve? One reason is that such measurements *don't* always "settle it." But the deeper reason is that trusting in measurements doesn't eliminate the need for judgment; it depends on a whole series of *prior* judgments, all of them potentially contentious. To mention but a few of them, we have to agree that the scale is in good operating condition, that the rocks aren't too heavy for it, that the theory of measurement on which the scale is based is correct, and that we aren't too drunk, dim-sighted, or prejudiced to read the numbers on the dial. We might even agree that one rock is heavier than the other, but later, after revisiting these judgments, change our minds. From difficulties like these, we don't conclude that weight is unreal. Neither should we say that beauty is!

Far from fictitious or false, loveliness is such a massive and bewitching reality that at times it threatens to undo us. And here is the thing about loveliness: Like that light from the Beloved's face, it seems to point beyond itself. The perishable sings to us of imperishability:

> Question the beautiful earth; question the beautiful sea;
> question the beautiful air, diffused and spread abroad;
> question the beautiful heavens; question the arrangement
> of the constellations; question the sun brightening the day

by its effulgence; question the moon, tempering by its splendor the darkness of the ensuing night; question the living creatures that move about in the water, those that remain on land, and those that flit through the air...question all these things and all will answer: "Behold and see! We are beautiful." Their beauty is their confession.[6]

The word "confession" at the end of this passage is meant literally, for Augustine, its author, views beautiful things as wordless, poignant witnesses. He asks, "Who made these beautiful transitory things unless it be the unchanging Beauty?" Let us put off trying to answer his rhetorical question for now. At the moment I am not concerned to say whether these beautiful transitory things really do confess something beyond themselves; it is enough for the argument that they seem to. Just for now, consider it an illusion if you wish.

For because of this inescapable seeming—whether or not it is grounded in reality—these beautiful things will never be enough for us no matter how much of them we have. The greater the beauty, the greater the sense of a still greater beauty beyond, behind, or above them. I can spend all day looking at the beautiful earth and sea, until I no longer want to. I can tire myself out feeling the breath of the beautiful air, diffused and spread abroad. I can take in so much of the arrangement of the constellations that I need to go indoors and catch my breath. Yet the longing for that *something more* will follow me inside. It may hide itself from me for days on end, and then strike me like a blow.

I hope I am not misleading anyone by speaking so much about the face of the moon and of the beloved. Although the mysterious longing for *something more* can be stirred by those things, it can be stirred by all sorts of other things too. In fact, it can be stirred by almost anything, depending on one's susceptibilities. In certain moods, the sense of the significance of a grain of dust can hit like the blow of a hammer. Some, like Aldous Huxley, have even been known to artificially stimulate the sense of significance by using drugs, foolish as that is.

In every one of these cases, we suffer a tendency to mistaken identification, a confusion between some ordinary desire, on one hand, and on the other what we may call the transcendental thirst. I may be moved to my depths by contemplating the miracle of water, but although taking a sip may quench my physical thirst, it will not quench my transcendental thirst. I may be transported by the sight of great works of art, and while I may have joy in possessing them—a joy, by the way, that fades—I will still be haunted by that astringent longing for *something* that I first thought must be the works themselves, or at least the beauty of them, but is really something else. The desire for each thing can be satisfied by that thing, yet the desire of which I speak will persist.

I do not say that everyone will recognize this experience. I do think that everyone has it—whether or not he accepts where the argument is going.

For the argument is going somewhere, and I may not want to go there. I may tell myself that my problem lies only in *not yet having enough* of whatever I want. For example, if the inexpressible desire is inflamed in me by great works of art, I may think my problem is that I don't want merely an object of beauty, or even a houseful of objects of beauty—but all beauty! And "all beauty" is a pretty good description of the transcendental longing, at least as some people experience it.

But I will not have "all beauty" even if I do possess every beautiful thing that there is. Beauty isn't an aggregate. It isn't an agglomeration. It isn't an attribute of a heap.

If beauty doesn't move you, think of what does. The mistake that the aesthete makes about having all beauty, some rich men make about having all wealth; some tyrants make about having all power; some wantons make about having all women (or all men); some scientists and philosophers make about having all knowledge of laws and of principles. But it doesn't matter how much in this world we possess, or what we possess. It is never enough. It cannot be enough.

Let there be no misunderstanding: I am not merely saying that desire is infinite, as some economists say. It is closer to the truth to say that what we desire is *The Infinite*—and even this is misleading if "The Infinite" is taken to mean merely "more and more and more." The problem is not just that however much I have of what I want, I want still more of it—in fact, not everyone does have that problem! Rather it is that whatever I have and however much I have, I want something else, something in some sense *beyond*, something that by its very nature lacks the limitations of the goods we meet in the ordinary course of life.

But if this is true, then nothing in our natural experience can make us fully happy. Not even virtue plus "everything else" can lull all desire, for while things that are *this* can refract the strange longing for *that* and fan it into flame, they can never quench it. Things in this world cannot be more than they are. No creature of nature, no fruit of our minds, no work of our hands will suffice. If there is no *beyond*, if it is all a delusion, then we are just out of luck.

# CHAPTER 17

# The Imperfect Happiness to Which These Reflections Point

"Has not man a hard service upon earth?"[1]

N
o doubt there are many other goods we might have investigated—does happiness lie in *this*, in *this*, or in *this*?—but the drift of the argument is clear. Let's summarize. Above all else in this life, happiness needs virtue, for whatever other goods we may possess, they will scarcely be good *for us* apart from virtue. But contrary to the view of the Stoics, virtue alone is not sufficient for happiness. Happiness requires not only virtue but also a sufficiency of the other necessary things: good character, yes, but also good fortune.

"So, then, these are the blessings men wish to win."[2] Yes, we might call this the Worldly Wise Man's view of happiness. Cultivate virtue and hope for luck.

From one point of view, it's a pretty good answer. There is a certain heft to it. Many people would more or less agree with it if it were presented to them. Perhaps most would. It not only tells us how to guide ourselves and what to aim for, but also how to teach the young and how to provide for their futures.

But from another point of view, the answer is pretty shabby. Such happiness is radically incomplete. It is fragmentary, vulnerable, and imperfect. Did we work through all these pages, did we do all this work, just for *that*?

Let's explore a little further. Through discipline we can develop virtue, and through virtue we can make the best of such fortune we have—but virtue doesn't *produce* good fortune. Good character equips us to deal with the other goods, to use them in the best possible ways—but it isn't *itself* those other goods. And although the virtues help to defend against pain, penury, sickness, loneliness, and many other evils, they cannot abolish them.

Besides, we don't just want to have the virtues, we want to exercise them. It isn't just that we need virtues to know how to deal with other goods that we have. It's also that we need some of those other goods for the virtues that we do have to work with. Am I to be generous to my friends? Then I must have something to give them. Am I to be prudent? Then I must have responsibilities that I can carry out well. Am I to be just? I must have responsibilities, opportunities for the exercise of justice. Ever since Aristotle, such things have been called the "equipment" of virtue. They are virtue's instruments, its tools, the things that it works with to build a good life.

And what if we lack this equipment? Perhaps you have good character but fall into dreadfully poor health. The virtue of temperance will surely help you preserve health, but it can't guarantee it. Sickness, injury, and infirmity may strike you no matter how moderately you eat and drink. Augustine asks, "Is the body of the wise man exempt from any pain which may dispel pleasure, from any disquietude which may banish repose? The amputation or decay of the members of the body puts an end to its integrity, deformity blights its beauty, weakness its health, lassitude its vigor, sleepiness or sluggishness its activity—and which of these is it that may not assail the flesh of the wise man?"[3]

Or perhaps you have the virtues requisite to true friendship, but no friends. "So many qualities are indeed requisite to the possibility of friendship," writes Samuel Johnson, "and so many accidents must concur to its rise and its continuance, that the greatest part of mankind content themselves without it, and supply its place as they can, with interest and independence."[4] Perhaps there are many who might otherwise have been friends, but who are so far separated from you in outlook that there is nothing of substance that you can share or discuss with them. Perhaps you discover that the good things in your life isolate you, either because others envy your good fortune or because so many people feign friendship in order to get something from you—and so good fortune may not be so good even if you do have good character. There may even be a shortage of persons in your society who are capable of friendship. You may live under a political regime that encourages citizens to inform on each other, so that friendship is a prohibitive risk. You may have and cultivate deep friendships, only to find that they are lost or impaired through misunderstandings beyond your control. Johnson says, "Those who are angry may be reconciled, those who have been injured may receive a recompense; but when the desire of pleasing and willingness to be pleased is silently diminished, the renovation of friendship is hopeless; as, when the vital powers sink into languor, there is no longer any use of the physician."[5]

Besides, no one's fortune is *entirely* good. Inevitably we suffer defeats and discouragements. Early death means wasted promise; long life means only long old age. We grow old, our powers fade, and we die. Those we love disappear one by one. If you are virtuous you will have a greater ability to endure suffering, yet that does not make it something other than suffering. Even having good character and good fortune, you may be deluded about the ultimate meaning of life—and it would seem a little odd to count knowledge of the meaning of life as part of "good fortune." Someone might suggest that cultivating good character and making the best of our lot is the only meaning there is. But if it really is the only meaning, then why does it seem that there must be another, and why do we keep looking for it?

Moreover, not even the golden combination of good character plus good fortune will satisfy the transcendental longing we have discussed. However good the virtues are, however good the other goods of life are, at times it seems as though there is some great point they are massively missing. What point is that? They cannot tell us. The virtues and the other goods are mute.

So suppose you have virtue. Suppose that for now you have the good fortune to possess a sufficiency of health and external possessions. Suppose that for now you have friends with whom to share this good life. Suppose that even though you may not know the ultimate meaning of life, at least you know some things, and you are not chasing delusions.

That is a great deal. It is nothing to sneeze at. You may certainly be said to have a share in happiness. We can even say that you have that approximation to happiness that can be had in this life. From the Worldly Wise Man's point of view, that *simply is* happiness. But is it? Not by a long shot.

# PART THREE

## *Starting Over*

"I was thinking that I had made an end of the
discussion; but the end, in truth, proved to be
only a beginning."[1]

# CHAPTER 18

## Why Shouldn't We Settle for Imperfect Happiness?

"For such a falling short, and for no crime,
We all are lost, and suffer only this:
Hopeless, we live forever in desire."[1]

"What do you want, egg in your beer?"[2]

So far, reflection on universal experience has revealed universal disillusionment. Whatever in our natural experience we pursue as our ultimate consummation, we are disappointed, for it cannot fulfill us. In one sense, desire can certainly be satisfied, for with good luck, we can attain and possess whatever we pursue in the belief that our happiness lies in it. Yet in another sense, desire cannot be satisfied, for even when we get what we pursued, we still suffer desire. A certain something whispers to us that it was not what we really wanted.

Through history the human race has come up against and rediscovered this disillusionment many times. The philosopher Giacomo Lodovici points out three possible negative responses to it: Fanaticism, despair, and resignation.[3] As he rightly explains, a positive response is also possible, but first let's explore these three negative possibilities.

Suppose I choose fanaticism: I remain in denial. I tell myself that the problem is just that I don't yet have enough of these partial goods, so that I seek more and more of the same sorts of thing. This is futile, because the problem is not quantitative. It lies not in the amount of these goods, but in their nature. Not even the greatest possible quantity of partial satisfactions adds up to total satisfaction; indeed, too much of them makes them pall even sooner than otherwise. The compulsive womanizer does not get more satisfaction from all that sex, but less. The glutton gets less from his food; the plutocrat, from his money; the tyrant, from his power. The fanatic always demands a greater satisfaction than his satisfactions can give. Even intellectual enjoyments pall. Perhaps I have become the perfect master of some field of learning, but as the jaded sage of Ecclesiastes wrote, "of making many books there is no end, and much study is a weariness of the flesh."[4] Even books and study about happiness.

Suppose that instead I despair. Telling myself that the hope for complete satisfaction is baseless and nonsensical, I try my best to cast hope to the winds. *I will stop wanting to be happy!* But this is merely our old acquaintance, annihilation, come around again in different dress. We first met it in the guise of the paradoxical claim that happiness lies in giving up all desire. The new, more consistent version claims that we must give up even the desire for happiness itself. If I may borrow a remark made by William James in a somewhat different context, this response produces a horror kindred to a nightmare, but with one difference: In a nightmare I have desire to act, but no power. Here I have power to act, but no desire.[5]

Or suppose I elect resignation. I will take what I can get. If frustrating partial satisfactions are all I can attain, very well, then I will settle, or try to settle, for frustrating partial satisfactions. As Hobbes wrote, "[T]here is no such thing as perpetual tranquillity of mind, while we live here; because life itself is but motion, and can never be without desire, nor without feare, no more than without sense."[6] Perhaps this is what Thoreau was recommending when he complained that "the mass of men lead lives of quiet desperation," for he thought they wouldn't be so desperate if only they didn't want so many things.[7] No doubt we do want too many things, but there is a kind of desperation in "settling" too. Perhaps I can be excused for repeating another anecdote. One day in a graduate seminar one of my students argued vigorously that the sole meaning of happiness is pleasure. I couldn't help noticing that the issue was not just theoretical for her. Her voice had an edge like a saw.

"Don't you think happiness must be more than pleasure?" I asked.

"Why?"

"Because no matter how much pleasure one enjoys, it always leaves something to be desired."

"There isn't any such thing as perfect happiness," she said with annoyance, "just more and less."

"But don't we grade things 'more' and 'less' in relation to a standard?" I asked. She agreed that we do.

"But the standard for 'more' and 'less' happiness is complete fulfillment," I continued. "More means closer to it, less means further away. So if there weren't such a thing, even in principle, then there couldn't be degrees of it either."

"But there *are* degrees of it," she protested.

"Then in principle, there must be such a thing as perfect happiness," I answered. "Even if we don't have it. Even if we don't know what it is."

Bitterly, she exclaimed, "The reason we don't know what it is, is that there's no such thing. The fact that we always want more is just the way things are. If we're disappointed, we just have to get over it."

I was reminded of Thomas Aquinas's doctrine that the ultimate goal of human striving would not be the ultimate goal if something yet remained to be desired.[8] It was as though my student had read that teaching, but drawn the wrong conclusion. She was determined to pitch her tent on a plain of salt. *I will not be burned. I will not be moved. I will not be taken in.*

Is it possible to experience disillusionment about partial and finite satisfactions, yet not take any of these negative attitudes? Confronted with the brittleness and frangibility of the good, is it possible *not* to go into denial and become a fanatic, *not* to sink into despair, and *not* to settle? If this should turn out to be possible, then disillusionment might even turn out to have been a good thing. For by calling attention to an error, it would have aroused the desire to find a way around it.

And this is indeed how it is. The temptation to fall into these attitudes arises from forgetting that each of the finite and limited goods in our natural experience derives whatever goodness it has from some unlimited and as yet undiscovered good that it reflects and anticipates, as charm anticipates but is not the same as true beauty. Consequently, just as someone might expect too much from charm, someone may ask more of any of these limited goods than they can give, forgetting to look beyond them to that greater good that transcends them.

Very sweet, says the skeptic. But why should I believe that limited goods *are* reflections and anticipations of something more?

We saw one reason above. It doesn't even make sense to speak of something partial except in comparison to something whole. That whole exists at least in our minds. Could it also exist in reality?

The answer is yes. In fact, it has to exist in reality, because it is nonsense to think that my nature contains a desire for something that cannot be had *even in principle*. The classical thinkers said that nature makes nothing in vain—that nothing in nature is for nothing. In our own flatter idiom, we might say that everything in us has a function, and "everything" includes our natural desires. They are always *for* something. I am not saying, of course, that every *specific* thing that I desire is within my grasp. If I desire ice cream that tastes like the number seven and is brought to me by fairies whenever I curl my toes, I will be disappointed. But the *generic* object of every natural desire must exist. I naturally desire food in general because food is a real thing that human life requires; if there were no such thing as food, then there would be no such desire. I naturally desire friends because friendship is a real thing and I need that too; if there were no such thing as friendship, then I would not have that desire either. The function of natural desire is to point the way toward satisfaction, and no natural desire exists unless its satisfaction is possible.

Someone may suspect that just now I have said something religious, in the sense of requiring faith. I will in a moment, but I haven't yet. In the meantime I would encourage anyone who thinks that I have said something religious to reconsider what he means by "religious," for we have arrived at our conclusion by reasoning, not by faith.

Some people offer a different objection: that joy lies in the seeking, not the having. They are talking through their hats. True, certain goods can be possessed only in the quest for other goods; for example, the keen intensity of hunting can be possessed only in the hunt itself. But after all, what we are hunting is the quarry—we are not hunting the hunt. We may enjoy preparing a meal, but there would be no relish in preparing one that no one would eat. We may enjoy the competition of a game, but if we were not trying to win, there would be no game to enjoy. We may enjoy learning, but the delight of gaining knowledge is in service to the delight of the knowledge itself. As Chesterton remarks, "The object of opening the mind as of opening the mouth is to shut it again on something solid."[9]

But if for every natural desire there is some possible satisfaction—and if, as we have learned from experience, nothing within our natural experience can fully satisfy our desire, then doesn't it follow by sheer logic that desire points beyond natural experience? That we must go, so to speak, out of this world? And I am not thinking of Mars.[10]

This, I concede, is a startling result. If the reader wishes to call my claim religious *now*, he may, since whatever lies beyond nature is by definition supernatural. Yet even if the conclusion suggests something religious, the argument itself is not religious, at least not in the sense of requiring faith. For we have arrived at the conclusion logically and empirically, without the use of any religion's revelation, creed, or scriptures. Not that we might not come to that too. But we haven't yet.

CHAPTER 19


## Is Happiness Something We Feel, We Have, or We Do?

"What is it, what, what, what is it, what is it."[1]


I n the first part of the book we asked whether happiness lay in
this or that—in power, say, or in being noticed. Since we are
starting over, let's ask instead what *kind* of thing it is. Is happiness or fulfillment an emotion, a condition, or an activity? Is it something we feel, something we have, or something we do?

Certainly happiness can't be a *bad* feeling. And we have already
seen that it isn't the same thing as pleasure or so-called positive feelings. We don't seek good things in order to have good feelings; rather
we have good feelings because we have attained good things. Suppose
I were able to hypnotize myself so that I *seemed* to experience the
pleasures of love, of friendship, of knowledge, without actually loving
anyone, without having a single friend, and without knowing anything at all. Wouldn't that rather miss the point? Or suppose I were
to cherish only good feelings and view my marriage merely as a way
to have them. Would I really be experiencing the happiness of marriage at all? The exultant joy of my marriage lies not in cherishing

joy as such, but in cherishing my wife and my partnership with her—*which is joyful.*

If happiness is neither a bad feeling nor a good one, then it isn't a feeling. But if it isn't a feeling, then what else could it be?

A great many people consider happiness to be a condition, like health, or a property, like warm-bloodedness. There is something to be said for this idea. For example, some think of happiness as the condition of fullness of life, and then say that life, in turn, is the property of being alive. Others think that we ought to seek to have all good things together (never mind, for the moment, whether they are all available within the natural order), and then say that happiness is the condition or property of enjoying them.

I don't exactly say that such views are wrong, but I think we will see that they are imprecise and somewhat misleading. To be completely happy is certainly to be fully alive and to enjoy all good things—but the exercises of life and enjoyment are not things that happen to us. They are things that we *do.* They are activities, or operations. If we call them conditions at all, we must insist that they are active conditions, like speaking or growing, not passive ones, like redness or oneness. A person in a happy "condition" is better described as involved in the *activity* of happiness: to use the ancient expression, the activity of living well and doing well.

Is it really plausible that happiness is an activity? Certainly the imperfect happiness that we have already investigated is an activity, for it lies in the exercise of the virtues—along with the good fortune that gives us opportunities to exercise them, for I can't practice generosity to my friends if I have no friends, I can't make proper use of material goods unless I have material goods, and so forth. But now we are addressing a different question: whether *perfect or complete* happiness—the understanding of which has so far eluded us—is an activity.

Various objections might be raised to this suggestion. One very old one is that since happiness would be my ultimate consummation, it would have to be something *in* me. Activities aren't ever in me, the skeptic says, because they always act upon or result in something *outside* me. For example, the activity of heating water or shaping a piece of clay acts upon the water or the clay, and the activity of house-building results in a house. Water, clay, and houses are not things within me. Since happiness takes place within me, but an activity always passes from me into something else, happiness isn't an activity.

The problem with this objection is the "always." It is true that many activities pass from me into other things. But many others, like understanding, do take place within me. Yes, by the activity of shaping a piece of clay into a statue, I am bringing something outside me into actuality and completeness. But by the activity of, say, understanding something, I am bringing something inside myself into actuality and completeness, in this case my knowledge. So we shouldn't say that if happiness is inside me, then it couldn't be an activity. Rather we should say that it would have to be an activity of the internal sort, like understanding—one that may *overflow* into external things but does not find its terminus there.

Another very old objection to the view that final happiness is an activity is that happiness in the complete and perfect sense would have to be something that continued without interruption or end. And isn't it the case, the skeptic asks, that every human activity suffers interruption, and that everything we do does come to an end? The most delightful conversation with my wife eventually concludes. It has to, because each of us has other things to do, not to mention having bodily needs, such as for rest. The process of writing this book is interrupted continually, and that sort of experience is familiar to everyone who has ever tried to accomplish anything. Even when there are no outside interruptions, we suffer internal interruptions. Perhaps I am praying, and my mind wanders. Perhaps I am preparing to lecture about something intriguing that Augustine of Hippo said, and I am distracted by the thought of the delicate small spider that so famously distracted him.

But notice what this objection proves and what it doesn't. Could any activity that starts and stops, that breaks up into pieces, and that suffers interruptions, be considered perfect happiness, leaving nothing to be desired? No, of course not; the skeptic is right about that. Does any activity that we can accomplish *by our natural powers* continue without interruption and without end? No, he is right about that too. Then must we say that no activity *at all* can continue without interruption and without end? That does not follow; the objector has gone too far. His conclusion would follow only if it were impossible to make contact with whatever transcends our natural powers. From the fact that we can't transcend our natural powers *by an exercise of our natural powers*, it doesn't follow that they can't be transcended; all this shows is that we can't pull ourselves up by our own bootstraps. Is there some other way to get beyond them? Since we haven't yet investigated the matter, all we can say is that we don't yet know.

In fact, if we bear in mind the conclusion of the last chapter, we have excellent reason to go on and conduct that investigation. Nature makes nothing in vain, and if the inescapable natural longing for happiness were inescapably frustrated, then it would be in vain. So it is hard to reject the possibility that the longing for perfect happiness can somehow be satisfied, even if only by means "out of this world."

Slow down, says the skeptic. Maybe we moved too quickly in the last chapter. Maybe nature *does* make things in vain. What about tonsils? The appendix? Junk DNA? Didn't we all read in our schoolbooks that these and probably many other things have no function, no purpose, no use? I don't know whether we all did, but I did. But the schoolbooks were wrong; as it has turned out, these things do have functions and purposes. Among other things, the tonsils may play a role in the immune system, the appendix may preserve useful symbiotic bacteria, and although it is true that some stretches of DNA don't codes for proteins, the ones that don't are hardly "junk." They seem to perform a variety of other tasks, for example switching some of the other stretches on and off.

Besides, a strong but absolutely futile desire would not just be useless—it would be worse than useless. It would involve us in tempests of longing, seeking, and wasted energy for nothing. Neither in Aristotle's theory of natural teleology nor Darwin's theory of natural selection is there any place for such an expensive futility: according to Aristotle, it shouldn't exist in the first place, and according to Darwin, it should have died out. Yet the desire for *something else*, something other than we find in this world, is universal, immensely powerful, and shows no sign of dying out.

Still another objection to the suggestion that ultimate happiness is an activity is that happiness is one thing, while activities are numerous and diverse. The answer to this objection is a lot like the answer to the last one. The fact that activities are numerous does not prove that there is no single, unified activity of the human person in which happiness would consist. It only means that we haven't yet discerned what it is. "We haven't yet discovered P, so P must not exist" is not a very good principle of investigation. Rather we should say "If we have good reason to think P must exist, but we haven't yet discovered it, then let's look for it." When Enrico Fermi found good reason to think that there must exist a fundamental particle that doesn't possess mass—a "neutrino," as he called it—physicists began looking for it. Eventually they found it. In this respect, they study of happiness ought to proceed the way physics does.

But doesn't the very fact that we can't bring about perfect happiness by our own powers show that happiness couldn't be an activity? An activity is something that we do. How could happiness be something that we do, if we have no power to do it? Allow me to answer with a few analogies. I have no power to see distant galaxies, because my eyes are not strong enough. However, if my visual power is augmented by a telescope, then I can. Should we say, "in that case, you're not performing the activity; the telescope is"? No, because the telescope isn't seeing. I am. If I don't look through it, no seeing takes place. We don't say that just because I need the help of the telescope I am not really seeing. We say I am really seeing, with the help of the telescope.

Many activities are like this—we can do them, but only with help. I may be unable to digest milk proteins on my own, but do fine if I take an enzyme supplement. I may be unable to know by direct observation what happened at a time before I was born, but I can learn about it from witnesses I trust.

These analogies are not perfect because in each case the power that assists my natural power is another natural power: the telescope's natural power to magnify images, the enzyme's natural power to break down proteins, and the witnesses' natural powers to remember and recite what they have seen. The skeptic may remind me that even if other natural powers can assist my own natural powers, they cannot bootstrap my powers right out of the natural realm. And I agree.

But could some power that is already beyond the natural realm uplift me? We certainly haven't proven that this can happen. On the other hand, we haven't proven that it can't. At the present state of our inquiry, we don't know. With such high stakes, it would be foolish to rule out the possibility ahead of time.

But isn't the idea of something beyond the natural realm illogical? We are in danger of going down a rabbit hole of digressions here, but the question is important, so let's answer it as briefly as possible. Only in one case is it illogical to think that there could be anything beyond the natural realm: if we define the natural realm ahead of time as "everything that is." And that begs the question, doesn't it? We don't know that natural causes and effects *are* all there is. In fact, there is excellent reason to think that they *aren't* all there is, because nature is not what philosophers call a necessary being. It didn't have to exist at all; there might not have been any such thing. Something had to cause this whole magnificent ensemble of causes and effects to exist. So on one hand we have the natural order—and on the other hand whatever caused it to exist. Two things. The latter is not part of the former.

The standard objection to this reasoning is that if the universe needed a cause, then its cause would need a cause, and so on *ad infinitum.* But no, the logic of the argument is not that everything needs a cause, but only that what are called contingent things need causes: only things that *don't have to be* require an explanation for their existence. If the cause of the universe is what is called a necessary being, then it doesn't need an explanation for its existence. Something that *can't not* exist just exists.

And please notice that this argument is just as compelling whether we view the natural realm as a unitary thing, or view it, according to the current fashion, as a "multiverse" or set of many unitary universes. For in either case, we are asking the same question: Why is there something and not nothing? The only difference is that in one case the "something" is called a universe, and in the other it is a symphony of universes called a multiverse.

To close this digression about the natural realm and return to the main subject: even after we have addressed the objections to the suggestion that happiness is an activity, it still seems strange to many people to think of happiness this way. They think that happiness isn't something that a person *does,* but something that *happens* to him: "That lucky guy!"

But if we consider our experience carefully, I think we will find that we frequently confuse things that we do with things that merely happen to us. Consider love, for example. Properly speaking, love is an enduring and active commitment of the will to the true good of another person. It is something we carry out, something we exercise, something we do. Yet we speak of "falling in love" as though it were like falling off a cliff or being struck by lightning. It is not hard to see why we speak this way, because although I may come to love someone only gradually and for reasons that I understand, sometimes the process is very fast and mysterious. Just as I fall off a cliff suddenly, I may begin caring for my beloved suddenly. *Wham!* In the same way that I may not be able to explain why the lightning struck me, I may not be able to explain why I began caring for her. "What is this miracle?" I ask. Songs have been written about the abruptness of it; sonnets about the mystery of it.

And yet, on reflection, we see that these resemblances between things that we do and things that merely happen to us are far from complete. The differences are much greater. For even if I did begin to care for my beloved all in a flash, my exercise of this care is an activity, and an absorbing one. I consider what will please her, I console her in sorrow, I try to remove thorns from her path, I repent of my hurts to her, I make a special effort to exercise the virtue of patience toward her, and I avoid making myself merely an object of toleration to her. And even if I don't fully understand why I do care for her, it is I who care and not another. This care is not inflicted on me, but transpiring and growing in my will.

So it is with many things we do. Like the sweet labor of love, in some ways these activities are like things that just happen to us, but they are not like that in all ways. So it is, I suggest, with the sweet labor of happiness.

# CHAPTER 20

# If Happiness Is Something We Do, Then What Activity Is It?

"For I ask all men whether they would prefer to have joy in truth or in falsehood. They hesitate no more in preferring the truth than in wishing for happiness itself."[1]

Wе have reached a sensitive point. I am about to argue that consummate happiness must lie in union with God—in fact, that happiness lies in the mind's gaze upon Him, in His own being, in what He is in Himself.

Unacceptable! Isn't that what Christians say? If the argument converged on a Sufi or a Buddhist conclusion, perhaps no one would object. These days, Christianity arouses protests. Notice, though, that even though this chapter will arrive at something that Christians believe, it will make no use of Christianity to get there. So I promise those who suffer visceral responses to the claims of faith that for now, at least, their viscera are safe. I don't promise not to endanger their viscera later.

The argument can be stated in a few sentences, and the only reason for expanding them to the length of a chapter is to respond to a few inevitable objections. Not to *all possible* objections, of course. New objections can always be raised to any argument whatsoever; new objections can be raised to any of the replies to the objections. The inability to think of still more objections may prove that the objector lacks imagination, but it is not a reasonable test of an argument's cogency. There is no escape from the need to exercise judgment.

Let's get started, then. In the last chapter we concluded that happiness is an activity. What activity is it? The word *activity* is related to the word *actualize,* and this is no accident. An activity *brings into actuality* some power or potentiality that would otherwise be only latent. Eating actualizes or fulfills the nutritive power; breathing actualizes or fulfills the respiratory power. We don't just happen to have these powers; we have them for the sake of their actualization. Each of them is *for* something. So to ask, "In what activity does happiness lie?" amounts to asking "Of what power or powers is happiness is the actualization or fulfillment?"

The very idea that natural powers may have purposes that can be attained, fulfilled, or actualized is deeply objectionable to some people. In fact, denial of natural purposes is pretty well drummed into us today, because our education is so steeped in materialism. It is supposed to be unscientific to believe in natural purposes. In order to explain why this objection is wrong, let me address its three main variations.

One version of the objection is that attributing natural purposes to things is a form of animism, like attributing deliberation and will to a rock, a river, or the wind. But I am not doing anything of that sort. To say that the purpose of the heart is to pump blood is not to make the ridiculous claim that the heart has a will of its own and that its intention is to keep the blood moving; it is merely to say that the heart both accomplishes something *and exists to accomplish it.* Unlike a deliberating mind, the heart is not thinking about the matter. It only acts *as though* it were. We use the same word for purposes in minds and for purposes in things because they are analogous, not because they are identical.

Another version of the objection is that although thinking of inanimate things as having purposes may once have led to interesting discoveries, science has gotten beyond all that now. But science has not, in fact, gotten beyond all that. Fields as diverse as optics and quantum mechanics make extensive use of what physicists and mathematicians call "variational principles," according to which systems tend to behave in such ways as to minimize, maximize, or hold constant certain quantities. For example, a beam of light passing through a prism seeks the path that minimizes the optical distance, which is the physical distance multiplied by the angle of refraction. Materialists dislike saying that the light "seeks" the path of least optical distance, because the term "seeks" is suggestive of a mind with a will. To avoid that suggestion, they prefer to say that the prism "makes" the light bend. It is hard to see what they gain by this. If we are not allowed to use language that might remind us of minds, then the language of *seeking something* and the language of *making something do something* ought to be equally suspect! Let's just say that light beams, prisms, and other things act *as though* they had minds even though they don't, and let it go at that.

Still another version of the argument is not so much materialistic as skeptical; it says not that there aren't any natural purposes, but that we can't know them, because only the maker of something knows what it is for. I know the purposes of my own works, such as the house that I've built, because I know my own mind. I don't know the purposes of natural things, such as eyes, because the Creator made them, and how can I read His mind? But I don't need to read the divine mind to know what eyes are for. I only need to know (1) that eyes see, and (2) that I can't even explain why I have eyes in the first place without referring to this fact. The reason for the existence of eyes is to enable me to see.

We were asking, "Of what power or powers is happiness is the fulfillment or actualization?" Presumably it would be our *highest* powers. Why? Because those are the ones that define us. I am most myself, most in tune with my nature, not when I am employing the lower powers that I share with the plants and beasts, such as eating, growing, or receiving sense impressions, but when I am employing the higher powers that distinguish me from them, such as deliberating about what to do or trying to ascertain the truth about something. This is why, even though both our higher and lower powers are true aspects of us, we don't compliment ourselves for self-command when our minds obey our passions, but when our passions cooperate with our minds. And this is why, even though we are more than naked minds, we view the decisions and conclusions of our minds as the decisions and conclusions of our whole selves. The man who is ruled by his feelings and appetites is in bondage.

Against this view, three arguments are offered: (1) reason is not the highest power because it *cannot* rule the passions; (2) reason is not the highest power because it *should not* rule the passions; and (3) it doesn't matter which element of us rules, because nature does not know any "higher" or "lower." Let us consider these in turn.

We have already seen a proponent of the first objection in chapter 9: David Hume, who called reason "the slave of the passions" and said that it could never pretend to any other function than "to serve and obey them."[2] But as we also saw there, Hume's argument is circular: he first defined all impulses that affect the will as passions and then said that only passions can affect the will. The supposed tyranny of feelings is certainly convenient; it provides us with an excuse for doing whatever we want. When challenged about our choices, we need only say, "I can't help how I feel, and I feel I have no choice." But it is a fallacy.

The second objection—not that the passions inevitably do rule but that they *should*—had an apostle in the poet John Keats: "O for a life of sensations rather than of thoughts!"[3] And we all know how the galaxy was saved when Luke Skywalker finally followed the advice of Obi-Wan Kenobi, "Luke! Trust your feelings!"[4] Heaven forbid that he should have trusted his judgment. This idea that the feelings should rule has numerous variations, each proposing a different kind of feeling as the ruler. Moralists propose *moral* feelings; religious folk of the emotional sort propose *religious* feelings; hedonists, *pleasant* feelings; aesthetes, *beautiful* feelings; Romantics, *ecstatic* feelings; and transgressivists, *morbid or forbidden* feelings—transgressivism being the point to which all Romantics come if they follow the Romantic path to the end, for if the feeling that you crave comes from crossing normal boundaries, then eventually you will have to cross the boundaries of normal feeling. But the problem is the same in each case: the passions that are nominated as rulers are themselves in need of rule.[5] So the second objection is mistaken too.

The third objection was that it doesn't matter which element of us rules, because nature doesn't know any "higher" or "lower"—that such distinctions are imposed upon nature from outside. But are they? Plants have only such powers as growing and absorbing nutrition. Beasts have these but also additional ones, for example the power of perceiving things through their senses. Human beings rise still higher, for we have rational powers. Not only can we perceive things through our senses, but we can grasp universals—for example, we can know not just a good taste, but the *idea* of good taste, and in fact the idea of good in general. Moreover, not only can we seek things according to instinct, but we can deliberate. So the sensitive powers rank above the vegetative powers, but the rational powers are still higher. It makes no more sense to deny the reality of higher and lower powers than of higher and lower mountains.

Consider too that plants seek their ends automatically, without even knowing what they are seeking. Animals "know" their ends in the sense that they pursue them, but they do not know them in a reflective sense, for they do not even grasp the concept of an end. We not only pursue our ends but also *know that they are ends*—we experience them not just as felt impulses but as meanings, as rational purposes, as reasons for doing what we do. Rationality is more, much more, than being clever or knowing many things. One can even imagine a beast that is cleverer than we are, knows far more than we do, and can do many more things than we can—yet is not rational. For rationality takes the lower powers up into reason, brings them into partnership with reason, imbues them with sense and context. We seek not bare life, but a human life, which is a considered life. We not only respond to our inclinations, but regulate them, wonder about them, and inquire into them, just as we wonder about all things. Until we find their meaning—until we are in accord with this meaning through and through—we cannot be at rest.

Suppose, then, we agree that happiness must lie in an activity of our highest power, and that our highest power is reason. Is our work done? No, there is one step more, because our fulfillment would have to lie in the *highest* activity of our highest power, and reason has more than one activity. One of its activities is practical: we deliberate about and organize our lives. The other is contemplative: we also seek and reflect upon the truth. Which of these two is highest?

Practical reasoning may seem highest because, as we have seen, even the fragmentary and imperfect happiness of this life depends on the exercise of the virtues, and the virtue of prudence, or practical wisdom, is the one that sets all the other virtues in proper order.

That is nothing to snort at! But on closer examination, practical reason couldn't be reason's highest activity, for *doing* presupposes *knowing*. Even the most hard-headed person wants to organize his life in accordance with what is really true. Don't we in fact try to do so, even if we aren't always thinking about it, and even if our assumptions about the truth are wrong? If someone were to become convinced that his whole life had been based on a delusion, he would fall into despondency. That is the point of the quotation from Augustine that I placed as the epigraph to this chapter, for even though we profoundly desire joy, we are no more hesitant to prefer truth than we are to desire joy itself. Ignorance may produce the illusion of bliss, but ignorance is not bliss. Leave that to the cows and the sheep. We are men and women.

The curious thing about us is that we desire knowledge not just to guide our deliberation but also for its own sake. And it is more than curious, isn't it? In this desire lies much of the nobility of the human creature. "All men by nature desire to know," writes Aristotle. "An indication of this is the delight we take in our senses," he explains, "for even apart from their usefulness they are loved for themselves; and above all others the sense of sight. For not only with a view to action, but even when we are not going to do anything, we prefer seeing (one might say) to everything else. The reason is that this, most of all the senses, makes us know and brings to light many differences between things."[6]

Even shabby tabloid journalism exploits our desire to know truth. The *National Enquirer* catapulted itself to greater prominence in the 1980s by means of the advertising slogan, "Enquiring minds want to know." You would think that the tabloid's marketing experts had read Aristotle. More likely they were capitalizing on the obvious.

But just as our highest rational power is directed to *knowing*, not just doing, so some objects of knowledge are higher than others. Wouldn't it be the case, then, that the highest activity of our highest power would lie not in knowing the most trivial and base objects of knowledge, but its very highest and noblest objects—especially the truth about God? For what activity of our minds could be higher than to see God—to know Him as He is in Himself?

At this point another objection might be proposed, for it may seem implausible that happiness lies in *any* kind of knowledge if we understand knowledge as the grasping of abstractions, the way an intellectual knows the proof of theorem—which does, by the way, seem to be how the thinker Aristotle viewed the happiness of contemplation. Two different responses to this objection are possible. One response is that it underestimates the joy that those capable of understanding abstractions do take in grasping them, but I admit that most of us find this response unconvincing. It would make happiness very much the business of an intellectual elite, such as mathematicians or philosophers, and there are an awful lot of unhappy mathematicians and philosophers, aren't there?

The other response is more compelling. When we say that happiness is a kind of knowledge, we should be thinking not so much of mathematicians or philosophers, but of lovers. The happiness of knowing God would not be the happiness the intellectual has in knowing a theorem or abstraction, but rather the kind of happiness the lover has in knowing the beloved. But in this case, the knowledge would be perfect and all-consuming, and the beloved would be the infinitely lovable—the Divine Source of all good and beauty, the Origin of love itself. The vision of God would seize and consume us. And this response seems satisfying.

Even now I am not yet making a faith claim. The argument to this point is simply reasonable.

For consider: There *has to be* a First Cause, a First Reason. Otherwise we cannot explain why there is anything else. The village atheist who says, "Oh, yeah? If God created everything, who created God?" merely betrays his misunderstanding of the argument. Things that *don't have to be*, contingent beings, require causes; things that *have to be*, necessary beings, do not require causes. God is not a thing among others to be explained. He is that without which nothing is explainable. To reject Him, then, is to say that there don't have to be reasons for things, that in the end, nothing has to make sense.

Pagan mythology was more or less explicit about nothing making sense. It didn't picture the First Reason creating all things from nothing and then calling all things back to Himself; rather it pictured the gods themselves inexplicably coming from the void. Since everything was held up by nothing, ultimately nothing was held up at all. To believe in the First Reason is the very opposite of believing in that kind of god; this sort of God is the very precondition of things making sense.

And let us be very clear: No one who believes that things don't have to make sense has any business saying that anything at all is true or false, or that anything does or does not exist. For how would he know? Do not reproach me with chaos theory. What mathematicians call chaos is not things not making sense, or not possessing order. Rather it has to do with the limits of prediction in certain kinds of highly ordered systems. The study of such systems does not require the abandonment of reason.

And so at the end of this chapter we arrive at the conclusion that the beginning of the chapter foreshadowed. There is no higher activity than seeing God, knowing Him as the lover knows the beloved, face to face.

But there is another difficulty, a more serious one, to which we now turn.

# CHAPTER 21

# Can We Do It on Our Own?

*"Are thy wonders known in the darkness?"*[1]

Granted that happiness is the highest activity or fulfillment of our highest power—granted that this activity would lie in the highest and noblest object of knowledge—granted that that object is God—and granting God's reality, there is still a further question: *Can* we know him? It may seem that doing so would utterly exceed our abilities.

It would be very easy to misunderstand the objection I am raising here, so first let's consider some things I do *not* mean.

First, in saying that such knowledge would utterly exceed our abilities, *I am not suggesting that nothing about God is rationally knowable.* In fact, such a claim would be incoherent, for to know that nothing about God is rationally unknowable would be to know something about Him, wouldn't it? In fact, it would be to know a great deal about Him. We would have to know that even if He existed, He was infinitely remote, because otherwise one could not be so sure that knowledge about Him was rationally inaccessible.

We would have to know that even if He existed, He was unconcerned with human beings, because otherwise we would expect Him to have provided the means for humans to know Him. We would have to know that even if He existed, He was completely unlike the biblical portrayal of Him, in which He does care about us and has already provided such means.

So, in the end, the agnostic must claim to know quite a number of things about God, just to prop up his claim to not knowing any. The question for him is this: How can he rationally justify his claim to know all those things, since he also claims that he can't know them? It turns out that he is really saying that nothing about God is rationally knowable *except* the things that would have to be true for him to keep saying that nothing *else* about Him is rationally knowable. Why the exceptions? If the agnostic can't know the other things, how can he know these? It is all suspiciously arbitrary.

Second, *I am not suggesting that nothing about God is knowable except by means of faith or revelation.* In fact, without recourse to faith or revelation, this book has already commented on a few of the numerous reasons to believe that God exists. One is that for every natural desire there exists a possible satisfaction of that desire. Since there exists a profound natural longing that cannot be satisfied by anything in the natural order, that which satisfies it must exceed the natural order. Another is that if things that don't have to exist do need causes, then the entire ensemble of causes and effects must have a cause, and the First Cause couldn't be just one more contingent being, but would have to exist necessarily. As we have seen, to deny that contingent things need causes is to pull such a long thread from the fabric of reasoning that the whole garment comes unraveled. A third is that since unintelligent things cannot direct themselves according to their purposes, the purposeful order we see in nature must have been arranged by some being that does have intelligence.

Even if order among living things emerged from natural selection, as some people suggest, natural selection requires a universe that is already ordered a certain way in which to operate; and it is ordered that way, for as we have also seen, teleological principles are evident in the rest of the physical universe too. Besides, proponents of natural selection recognize that the process of selection operates only on self-replicating things, such as living organisms.[2]

Without elaborating, a few more of the reasons to believe that God exists might be mentioned just by way of illustration. There is the fact that reality has the amazing property of making sense to minds. Why should it? Unless this is just wildly good luck, which seems implausible, it must itself be the product of a Mind. Then there is the fact that there are moral laws. We couldn't have made them; we can't even change them. Therefore there must exist a moral lawmaker. I owe the shortest argument to philosophers Peter Kreeft and Ronald Tacelli: "There is the music of Johann Sebastian Bach. Therefore there must be a God." Kreeft and Tacelli remark, "You either see this one or you don't."[3] That understates its force, for either beauty is a real thing (which cannot be explained on materialistic terms) or else it is an illusion (which cannot be explained on materialistic terms either, since such an illusion would have no adaptive value for us).

Third, *I am not suggesting that reason tells us nothing about God but the bare fact of His existence.* The sorts of arguments we have been considering point not just to the bare existence of God, but to a great many of His attributes. He is the Creator. There is only one of Him, or else Creation itself would lack the coherence that we recognize in it. He is not a contingent but a necessary being—that is, He can't *not be*. He is the ultimate explanation of all else that is. He is not a blind "Force," as in *Star Wars*, but a personal Mind. He is the source of order, meaning, beauty, moral law, and good. Nor need we worry about whether He created evil too, because evil has no nature of its own, but can arise only by a disorder or lack in something good.[4] And since He is the ultimate object of longing, He is our *ultimate* good. All this, and much more, we can work out just by reasoning.

If I am not saying any of those three things, what then am I saying? Simply that there is an inconceivably great gap between knowing about God and *knowing God*. To know God is to be taken up into His own interior life. To know something about God may be crucial to knowing God, but in itself such knowledge may be as dead as chalk dust on a blackboard. The difference between *knowing* and *knowing about* is plain even in our everyday lives. I may know that Sandra exists. I may know that she is beautiful, that she is of such-and-such an age, and that she is so-and-so many inches tall. I may even know something about her virtues and talents. And yet even knowing all this, I may not know Sandra.

So it is with God, but far more so. By reason we can work out God's existence and many of His attributes, but knowing these falls far short of knowing God. The mind of the First Cause would be so much higher than our minds that His mind and our minds could be given the same name, "minds," only by analogy. Our minds perceive created things; His mind brings them about. Our thoughts have truth only by corresponding with how things really are; things are what they are only because they correspond with His thoughts. Since our minds are made for knowing things *within* the natural order, how can we possibly know that which lies above the natural order and causes it to be? We have no more conception of God's mind than a dog has of his master's—or than a character in a play has of the mind of the author. The latter analogy is not perfect, because the characters in a novel are not real persons but only depictions of persons.[5] Even so it has the merit of calling our attention to the vast gulf between a created being and the Uncreated Being by whom all created reality is made.

Or consider the difference between the good things we know in this life and the infinite Source of Good. Begin with just one of the goods we know: love. I know the love of biological fatherhood, but God is the creator of biology. I know the love of man and woman, but God is the creator of the sexes. I know the love of friendship, but God created in me the desire and potentiality for friendship with another of my kind. I may say that these loves must somehow reflect His love, or stand in analogy to His love, and I am sure this is correct. But although in most cases the gap between an original and a copy, between a thing and the thing to which it is compared, is finite, in this case it is infinite, and transcends the capacity of the copy to conceive.

Consider too that everything that we embodied beings understand is mediated to us through our senses. Water pours through my fingers, cools my skin, and slakes my thirst; from particular instances of sensing water, I form the universal concept "water." But how is God to be mediated to us through our senses? Is the Creator of surface and substance a thing to be felt? Is the Creator of light and color a thing to be seen? Seeing Him is another analogy—it means comprehending Him; I grasp realities with my mind and call it seeing them. But what will illuminate for me the very light by which I see?

It is beginning to look as though the desire of which we have spoken, the desire that cannot be satisfied by anything within the natural order, cannot be satisfied at all—because the natural order is the limit of what we can attain. We are no more likely to lift ourselves up to the beatific vision than to suspend ourselves in the air by pulling up on our trousers.

Is that our plight?

And there is another difficulty too. So far in this chapter we have been speaking as though the difficulty in knowing God were purely intellectual. For isn't knowing an activity of the mind? Yes, but knowing is not a technique like making soup or carving wooden whistles. We do not say that only the pure in heart shall make soup, but according to an ancient tradition, only the pure in heart shall see God.[6] I do not offer this tradition as something to be accepted on faith, but as something that commends itself to the mind. It is not merely possible or plausible, but strongly probable. For purity of heart is like clear vision. My eye cannot see if other things are in the way; in the same way, my mind cannot know God unless, with a single heart, I desire God. Aren't we all too well aware that our desires can be deflected and disordered by the attractions of lesser things?

Besides, if God is indeed good, just, and the author of goodness and justice, then wouldn't impure and disordered desires that oppose His own will be absolute barriers to knowing Him? The suggestion is not that nothing else but God should be desired or pursued, but than nothing else should be desired in preference to Him, or pursued in a way that interferes with pursuing Him. "Thou has made us for Thyself," wrote Augustine, "and our hearts are restless till they rest in Thee"[7]—one would think this would settle the matter. But even if our minds can rest nowhere but in Him, we may certainly *believe* that they can rest apart from Him. Or we may have weak wills and divided hearts, believing in theory that Augustine is right, and yet acting as though he isn't.

For on one hand is God, Whom I cannot perceive with my senses, or—apparently—fully possess in this life. On the other is the charming, shapely, and available married lady next door, whom I perceive all too well with my senses, and can possess, so she tells me, in the next sixty minutes. Looking honestly at the scale, God wins hands down. But if my senses put their heavy thumb on the other pan, what then? I may not even be looking at the pans. I may be murmuring to myself, like Scarlett O'Hara, "I'll think about that tomorrow."

My example should not be misunderstood. Though the lady next door is a carnal temptation, the disorder in my desires—the deflection from my ultimate good—does not have to be carnal. Consider the spiritual temptation of having no one to whom we must answer but ourselves. Atheists are fond of saying that belief in God is a crutch, a comfort for weak minds who find life too difficult. But disbelieving in Him can also be a crutch, a comfort for deluded minds who think that they will be freer if they are alienated from the Divine Source of their freedom.

Or consider the temptation of renown. In recent years we have seen numerous instances of scholars and scientists deliberately falsifying data for the glory of spurious discoveries. What could they have been thinking? How could they rejoice in the glory of recognition for what they knew to be false? Yet they did.

For yet another, consider the temptation to be dishonest in order to avoid calamity. Perhaps I have nothing to show for my research, but unless I come up with something quickly, I will lose my grant. I promise myself that *next* time I will be honest. But lies metastasize, because all knowledge is connected. To cover up the first lie, I must tell more lies. The greater the original lie, the more the covering lies take on a life of their own. Before long, deception mutates into self-deception, for to relieve the dreadful weight of lying to all those other people, I begin to tell lies to myself. Soon I must tell more lies to cover up those lies too.

"But I haven't done *those* things!" Maybe not. Then what things have you done? Would you wish your most secret thoughts to be audible to others, or the deeds that give you the greatest shame to be displayed on your forehead? "My life is an open book!" is a boast that can be made only by those utterly ignorant of themselves. Notwithstanding the fact that human effort can go a long way toward virtue, even the most exemplary among us are deeply flawed. G. K. Chesterton famously quipped that original sin is "the only part of Christian theology which can really be proved." He was not referring to the story in Genesis, but to the obvious fact that there is something wrong with us, "a fact as practical as potatoes."[8]

The disgrace of it all lies not in the baseness of human nature, but in its nobility. We trade solid gold for gilt paint. We honeycomb our hearts with desires that oppose our deepest longings. We demand to have happiness on terms that make happiness impossible. We have no excuse. Worst of all, we seem powerless to fix our own distemper.

Or are we?

# CHAPTER 22

## *Could We Ever Do It on Our Own?*

"But the serpent said to the woman, 'You will not die. For
God knows that when you eat of it your eyes will be opened,
and you will be like God, knowing good and evil.'"[1]

I n the previous chapter we concluded that human nature in its
present state is both intellectually and morally incapable of seeing God. Now the road forks. Down the right-hand fork, we
might ask whether assistance of some sort is possible from God Himself. Turning to the left-hand fork, we might ask whether we may be
able to assist ourselves—whether it may be possible to uplift our own
nature, without any help from Him at all. Earlier I compared this
possibility with lifting ourselves by our bootstraps. But could it be
that this dismissal was premature? Might some kind of bootstrap-
ping really be possible?

We might call the right-hand fork divine, the left-hand fork transhumanist. Since the transhumanist option has received so much
attention in recent years, let us consider it first. I assure those who
have never heard of transhumanism that I am not making all this up.

Now presumably, since the deficiency that keeps us back from
beatitude is both intellectual and moral, the transhumanist solution

would have to be both intellectual and moral. Not only would we have to change the nature of our intellects, we would also have to change the nature of our desires. On the one hand we would have to attain such godlike minds that human self-knowledge became the *practical equivalent* of the knowledge of God, whatever that may mean—and on the other we would have to redesign the rest of our nature so that we *determined for ourselves* the conditions of human flourishing. We would reconfigure our longings, no longer pining for what we could not have, like dogs howling at the moon. We would no longer have to be good; to put it another way, we would decide for ourselves what counts as good.

This fork in the road is not new. Our most ancient traditions not only speak of it, but warn of it. The best-known of them maintains that when confronted with this choice, the earliest humans yielded to the temptation to partake without permission of the "knowledge of good and evil" so that they would be "like God."[2] The outcome is represented as having been disastrous. But it seems that the lesson did not take, because according to another such legend, as soon as men learned to make buildings from bricks and mortar they resolved to build a tower "with its top in the heavens" in order to "make a name" for themselves and unite human strength so that they would never be scattered over the face of the earth. At a stroke, the story goes, their plans were reduced to futility and confusion, and they were dispersed over the earth so that the very thing they had hoped to prevent came about.

Stylish modern impatience with ancient literary devices such as talking snakes and towers reaching to the heavens misses the point of such warnings. The classical interpreters did not read the legend of Babel as meaning that we should not make tall buildings, but that we must approach God through humility rather than pride.[3] They did not read the story of the Fall as meaning that we should avoid conversations with reptiles, but that no created being is the measure of its own knowledge. God's thoughts originate reality and the finite possibilities of good that it contains; our thoughts can never do more than reflect that reality. The first humans may have thought that they could originate for themselves new and different measures of what is to count as good and evil, but they ended up learning only "the good they had lost and the evil into which they had fallen."[4]

As these traditions show, the temptation to thumb our noses at God and try to become gods ourselves is as old as the human race and continually recurs. Consider, for instance the ruminations of Friedrich Nietzsche, who thought all it takes to rise above the human level is disillusionment and strength of will. He was convinced that the belief in objectively true values—a real good and evil, a real right and wrong, even a real *reality*—was finally petering out. Not much belief was left in the tank. Soon it would run dry. The age of nihilism would begin.

One result of this emptiness would be the rise of the herd creatures he called the "last men," people who would no longer believe in anything or aspire to anything (and who therefore might believe carelessly in anything), but who would know, more or less, what they wanted: above all they would want their lives to be comfortable, safe, easy, and just like everyone else's.

Another result would be the rise of a few exceptional individuals who would in some sense be more than human, men who—instead of receiving values from a supposedly transcendent source, such as God—would create their own values, imposing them on those weaker than themselves. Creating their own values would be tantamount to creating their own reality, for since purposes are built into things, good can be what it is only if the rest of reality is what it is. In some unimaginable sense, Nietzsche thought, the various supermen would war among themselves over the question of whose values and "facts" would prevail. Finally, when some of them were able to impose a new order of reality, the specter of the abyss would retreat. Not, mind you, that the abyss *itself* would retreat. There would merely be no horror in it.[5]

Ironically, the sort of people who prattle about "creating their own values" have turned out to be exactly the sort of people whom Nietzsche despised as "last men." The would-be supermen turn out to live in herds, bleating *Free at last, free at last! True for you, but not for me!* Let each person have his own reality—right along with his own new car and entertainment center. If God is dead, then everything is hey, whatever. So the age of nihilism that Nietzsche prophesied has come upon us, but it is not, as he thought, a story of last men and supermen. It is only another chapter in the story of futile attempts to build towers "with their top in the heavens."

Consider today's high-tech transhumanists, who rely not on the will to power but on imagined future techniques of nanotechnology, biotechnology, and the cognitive and information sciences—tools with which, they think, we will one day be able to redesign and reconstruct our very nature. If we wish, we will be able to adjust people to their particular lots in life in order to "enhance" their performance and satisfaction. We can have file clerks who never get bored, laborers who never go on strike, and miners who prefer the heat, dust, and dark.

Perhaps it is not hard to see that such manipulations would not enhance but diminish us. Yet some people find this point difficult to grasp. Why, they ask, should anyone have to be a square peg in a round hole? But that is an odd way to put the question. Rather we should ask, why should all our corners be cut off? Wouldn't it be better to leave us alone and change the shape of the hole?

*No!* say the transhumanists. *Life could be more to our liking!* Everyone could be smarter. Everyone could be stronger. Everyone could be more musical. And why stop there? Everyone could live forever, even if that meant putting an end to having children, a point Europe has almost reached anyway. No one need ever become depressed, even if he had something to be depressed about. No one need ever suffer bad dreams, or pangs of conscience, no matter what he had done. No one need ever go mad from not knowing the meaning of his life, for our minds could be readjusted so we thought we knew it already, or didn't care whether we knew, or believed that there was none and didn't care about that either. War would come to an end, because nations would peacefully submit to whatever their programmers decided to have them submit to. Or war would *not* come to an end, but we would be adjusted to that too, and like it.

Transhumanists believe the superhuman future is inevitable. Suppose your children are the only ones in the school without brain implants for concentration on tests: You wouldn't want them to fall behind, would you? As two promoters of the hoped-for revolution explain in the *Wall Street Journal,* a publication not otherwise given to wild-eyed prognostication, "even if parents don't invest in brain implants, the military will." Challenging reluctant readers, they ask, "Who could blame a general for wanting a soldier with hypernormal focus, a perfect memory for maps and no need to sleep for days on end?" Chillingly, they add, "of course, spies might well also try to eavesdrop on such a soldier's brain, and hackers might want to hijack it." But the prospect isn't chilling *to them.* "The future doesn't belong to the fainthearted," they croon. "It belongs to the brave."[6]

The authors comment that DARPA, the Pentagon's Defense Advanced Research Projects Agency, is already looking into these matters. In fact, various government agencies and private sector organizations have been looking into them for decades. At a conference co-sponsored some years ago by the National Science Foundation and the Department of Commerce, papers were contributed not only by those two agencies but also by the Office of Science and Technology Policy, the National Aeronautics and Space Administration, the National Institutes of Health, the American Enterprise Institute, Hewlett Packard, and the Institute for Global Futures.[7]

Transhumanist ideology is even getting into the curriculum. On one occasion I accompanied the freshmen in one of my courses to a university event designed to help undergraduates choose majors. One of the speakers was an enthusiastic physics professor who boasted that someday we would be able to upload our minds into computers, thereby living without the limitations of physical bodies. This was his argument for choosing physics as a major. It was inconceivable to him that anyone wouldn't want to get in on the ground floor of such exciting developments.

If such things horrify you, the transhumanist replies that your horrors can be readjusted. He believes that what we call a human being is just a sophisticated mechanism; what we call its nature is merely its operating system; what we call its consciousness is only its executive function; and what we call its deepest longings are but the objectives built into its program. Fulfillment can therefore have no other meaning than continual success in attaining what our programming leads us most strongly and persistently to desire. In the spirit of the legends, we might say to the transhumanist that we cannot displace the Creator because we cannot reinvent our humanity. But the transhumanist will reply, *Why can't we?* Why can't we provide ourselves with an improved human nature, not this old Paleolithic hand-me-down, but a new one we make for ourselves? Rather than thinking of human nature as *what we are*, transhumanists think of our nature as a shackle on what we are—and what we are can be anything.

You may think that I am painting an exaggerated picture of what transhumanists want. Whether or not one cares for the idea of rewiring soldiers so that they don't have to sleep, it isn't the same as trying to become gods. Really? Becoming gods is an admitted goal of some transhumanists. Physicist and biotech entrepreneur Richard Seed boasted, "God made man in his own image. We are going to become one with God. We are going to have almost as much knowledge and almost as much power as God. Cloning and the reprogramming of DNA is the first serious step in becoming one with God."[8] Tulane University physicist Frank J. Tipler has gone even further, arguing that through the advance of science, intelligent species will *literally* evolve into God. Yes, he really says this.[9]

Three incoherencies lie at the murky heart of the transhumanist program. Two of them were pointed out several generations ago by C. S. Lewis, before transhumanism was a movement, before it had a name, when it was hardly more than a cloudy presupposition of certain ways of speaking about the future, when it did not even speak explicitly of man becoming God.[10] The third has to do especially with man becoming God, and therefore goes straight to the heart of the matter.

First: According to transhumanist ideology, the time has come for "man" to decide what "man" shall become. As Lewis pointed out, this language is misleading, for it is really a proposal for some men to decide what other men shall become. If some people are to be changed, then others must change them. Even in the most democratic version of the ideology, which bids us think not of military, industrial, political, or ideological imperatives but only of parents choosing to "enhance" their children, the present generation arrogates to itself the power to decide what portion of the human inheritance future generations will be allowed to retain.

Second: If we really have no essential nature—if human beings can be turned into anything—then there is no possible basis left for deciding what they should be turned into. For if the natural law itself can be rewritten, then how can any plan for rewriting it be better than any other? First we erase the slate, then we write on it. But a blank slate cannot tell you what should be written on itself. To give permission to redesign our minds and deepest longings is to say that the motives our minds and longings supply to us *now* should be set aside. Having set them aside, the redesigners could have no other guide for their actions than the impulses they happened to feel at the moment of making the plan.

Third, and most fundamental: The idea that a creature could evolve into the Creator, that dependent beings could turn into absolute Being, is so muddled that one hardly knows how to argue with it. It is like saying that if only my powers become great enough, I will someday become my own father and beget myself on my mother.

How have we become so confused about what a nature is that we have come to believe that we can make one? I do not suppose that proponents of this ideology can achieve what they desire. I do think they might do great damage by trying. The brave new technologies of the transhumanists would enable man not to transcend himself, but only to destroy himself. Humans, so-called, would be artifacts, made things, constructs, like television sets or digging machines. The engineers would dream of being God, and the rest of us would dream of being engineers. Always supposing that dreams had not been engineered out of us too.

And for what? All to forestall the necessity of relying on God to know God. It is like saying, "You need not drink water. Whenever you are dry, take this pill. It will produce the illusion of drinking and suppress your thirst." But what if the pill works perfectly? Then one dies of dehydration: a perfectly desiccated, smugly self-satisfied mummy.

# CHAPTER 23

# *What Kind of Help Would We Need?*

"More light! More light!"[1]

L et's take stock of our conclusions so far. To be completely happy—to enjoy not just the fragmentary and imperfect happiness of the present life, but complete and utter fulfillment—we must see God as He is in Himself, behold Him with our minds. For this to be possible, our minds must be lifted above their natural powers, which are sufficient only for knowing created things, not for beholding their uncreated cause.

Moreover it seems that we must seek this ultimate goal with a pure heart and a single gaze. All other desires would have to be set in order by the sovereign desire; we would have to be cleansed, not of all other motives, but of any that would compete and distract from it.

But we cannot uplift our intellects beyond their natural limits, and we cannot heal the disorder of our desires. We would therefore need help from God Himself.

If He would give it.

People speak of many roads to God, but so far as I am aware, only one faith tradition speaks of the possibility of divine help in just this way. I am speaking of biblical religion, both Old and New Testament, culminating in the sacrifice of the God who took our burdens upon Himself so that we could be relieved of them. St. Peter even links the two requisites of complete fulfillment that we have discussed, when he remarks that through the promises of Christ His followers can "escape from the corruption that is in the world because of passion"—that is, be healed of the disorder of their desires—and become "partakers of the divine nature"—that is, be taken into the mystery of His interior life.[2]

This leaves us with a problem. If the tradition in question is true, it is excellent news. On the other hand, it presents itself not as a human invention or discovery, not as yet another theory worked out by philosophers proposing yet another way by which man reaches up to God, but as a divine gift by which God Himself reaches down to man. Obviously, if that is really true—if it really is a divine gift, something that our reasoning could not have worked out by itself—then we would be unable to ascertain whether it were true just by reasoning. We would have to lay aside the method we have been following all through this book.

Or would we? For the resources of reasoning alone are not yet exhausted. We can still ask reason about *whether it could be reasonable* to trust information that purports to come from beyond our power to attain it.

Let's tackle these difficulties one by one. In the next chapter I will consider in what sense faith may cooperate with reason—and in what sense it requires a step beyond it. Is it reasonable to accept help from beyond human reason, or is it blind and irrational? But in the present chapter, I will consider just what the tradition proposes that we believe: first, about the vision of God Himself, and second, about the healing of our interior disorder.

What does the tradition suppose the vision of God to be? It admits that not a great deal can be said about it: the faithful have only flashes and glimpses of God's countenance in this life. As St. Paul says, "For now we see in a mirror dimly, but then face to face. Now I know in part; then I shall understand fully, even as I have been fully understood."[3] Faith, in other words, is not direct knowledge, but only a foretaste of knowledge.

Obviously, then, we can't say "in seeing God, this is what we would see." But at least we can clarify some things about what it would and would not be to see Him.

First we must be very clear about what an enormous gap such a vision would close, and in what sense it would close it. The tradition maintains that God has already given us the astonishing gift of bearing His image. We are not like the plants or the beasts. In our finite powers to reason, love, and freely choose, we resemble Him, yet the difference between the original and the image remains infinite. God isn't the same as me, He isn't a part of me, and He isn't a "higher" me. I'm not the same as Him, I'm not a part of Him, and I'm not a "spark" or "splinter" of Him. Nor will I ever be. He doesn't depend on anything else, because He is what everything else depends on. He can't be explained by anything else, because He is what everything else must be explained by. He is unutterably beyond me.

To know Him would not be like knowing a sum in a workbook, or even the central theorem of a geometry book. In the vision of God, our minds would be taken up, with consuming intimacy, into the vastness of His own life. This would be true knowledge, far closer than I know my wife or dearest friend, unimaginably closer than I know myself, in its finite way like the way He infinitely knows me, personally, calling me by name. Even so my knowledge would not *encompass* the divine life, because nothing at all can make a finite mind like mine infinite like His. God encompasses what He is in the very act of understanding it; but although my mind might be uplifted to see what He is, I would not encompass what He is. To comprehend Him in that sense—to intellectually take in His infinity—one would have to be God Himself, which is impossible for us.

It follows that the vision of God is not complete in the sense that those enjoying it understand God's being so fully that there is nothing more to be known. No finite being attains to that. In this sense our knowledge is not and cannot be perfect. Yet in another sense it can be. For rather than merely knowing about God, they know God. And because, in this consuming experience, they behold Him as He is in Himself, they are satisfied.[4]

And what does the tradition propose with reference to the healing of our disorder? More can be said on this question than on the previous one, because the healing begins in this life.

God, having made us free, will not heal our disorder without our assent. Therefore, everything depends on the *yes*, the willing affirmation that the patient gives to the divine physician, for unless the patient is reconciled with the surgeon, nothing else can be done. How does this come about? Nothing I can offer in atonement for my moral failures is sufficient, but an atonement has been offered by God Himself on my behalf. The tradition claims that by vicariously sharing in the death and resurrection of Christ, I am able to die to myself and live in Him, something I could never have done on my own. Thinkers in the tradition have offered a number of theories of how the atonement works, but they all affirm that it does.

To speak of Christ may seem a little too concrete for comfort—must we be so definite?—but the tradition does not concede that there are many ways to God. There are many religions, and they are not all wrong about everything, but for the sickness of alienation, only one medicine has been provided.

If the patient—let us say it is me—continues to cooperate with the divine physician instead of pulling loose or struggling against the treatments, then the work of putting my thoughts, emotions, and desires in proper order can proceed. An essential element in the treatment is that I come to realize more and more clearly and sharply that God Himself is the supreme good from whom all created goods I desire come, and for the sake of which they all exist. Although some ways of pursuing these lesser goods can be directed to the supreme good that is Himself, others cannot.

But as the treatment continues, a series of changes ripple and cascade through me. Not all of this will be visible to others. Perhaps very little will be. We must remember that before the treatment begins I am cut off from the divine life, morally and spiritually sick, and dying. Yet a great deal takes place.

For example, although even apart from God I would have been able to develop a certain degree of moral discipline just by working at it, I would have eventually met a wall; everyone does. When I find myself doing the wrong I do not want to do and not doing the right that I want to do, I am now able to turn to His grace for assistance.

Speaking of grace, certain supernatural virtues depend on grace for their very existence. Chief among these is divine love. Apart from God, I may love my wife with natural love and affection, but I will fail in that supernatural charity that enables me to see that since she is made in His image, the only true way to love her for her own sake is to love her "for His sake"—to participate in His love for her, which is so inconceivably greater than my own. This possibility is now offered to me.

Trust in God restores confidence in conscience. If I do not believe that He made us, then it is almost impossible to resist the suspicion that the authority of conscience is an illusion—that whatever we think about right and wrong is but the meaningless and purposeless result of a process that did not have us in mind. What could a ragtag collection of impulses and inhibitions left over from the accidents of natural selection have to teach us? Better to be done with it! But if conscience is an emissary of the Creator, matters stand otherwise.

Such trust in the Creator of conscience also makes it possible not to despair when conscience accuses. Only a person can forgive. Consequently, apart from Him the moral law will seem not a gift, but a harsh accuser with a heart of rock. When I have done wrong, I will long to drown out its voice. The greater my determination to do so, the worse I am likely to become. For example, having treated you badly, I may soothe my conscience by convincing myself that you deserved it—and then, believing it, I may treat you still worse. I may even tell myself that the solution to the problem of guilt lies in pills, or in the theory that there is no such thing as guilt. But if behind the law stands its Author, then when conscience does confront me, I can submit to the grace of a change of heart and return to Him. At last I can experience the moral law not as a stone that breaks my foot, but as a step on which to stand and rest.

Moreover, if I cooperate with God I am relieved of the urge to do evil in order to make things turn out right. It is all very well to say, "Do the right thing and let God take care of the consequences," but this counsel will hardly seem convincing unless I am confident of a God who will one day bring everything to justice and wipe the tears from the eyes of the oppressed. By contrast, if I am fully convinced that He is in command, then I am no longer tempted to play God myself.

Confidence in the promises of faith also restores courage when we find ourselves in moral difficulties. Apart from Him, I will constantly seem to find myself in dilemmas in which no course of action is innocent. I will be tempted to agree with those philosophers who say that "dirty hands" are merely a condition of human existence, something we shouldn't fret about. But the tradition promises that if we are faithful to God, then He is faithful to us: "He will not let you be tempted beyond your strength, but with the temptation will also provide the way of escape, that you may be able to endure it."[5]

Ah, but there is a problem. Before reaching this chapter, we proceeded by reasoning—but now we have brought in claims of faith. Can it be reasonable for humans to believe something from beyond human reason?

# CHAPTER 24

# How Can We Get That Help?

"Test everything."[1]

T he whole point of revelation is that it exceeds what we could
have figured out for ourselves. But can it be reasonable to
submit to such help?

Certainly it is reasonable to submit to help from beyond *my own*
reason. I don't know tensor calculus, but I would be a fool not to
accept the results of the calculations of someone who does. The case
of revelation is a little different, because I must accept on faith certain
things that cannot be found out by *any* human reasoning, not just
my own. Yet even here we are speaking of the communication of
information by a Mind, one that is greater than ours.

A reasonable person would ask five things about revelation:
whether it is possible, necessary, likely, authentic, and confirmed.

Now it is certainly reasonable to consider revelation *possible*,
because although its truth cannot be philosophically demonstrated,
the reality, power, wisdom, and goodness of God Himself can be. It
is reasonable to consider it *necessary*, because even though we have

a natural inclination to seek the truth about God, our unassisted finite minds could never know His own mind. And it is reasonable to consider it *likely* because He who gave us the inclination to seek Him must desire that we find Him.

Is it reasonable to consider revelation *authentic*? This point is stickier, but the record of revelation, including events that are difficult to explain apart from divine intervention, is well attested by witnesses who are not easily discredited. Some people object to the miraculous on principle, but it is hardly cricket to say that extraordinary claims require extraordinary evidence—and then rule out extraordinary evidence.

Finally, is it reasonable to consider revelation *confirmed*? This point is sticky too, but assent to the revelation is accompanied by the experience of grace. Granted, we are not speaking of knowledge that can be confirmed from the outside. But consider an analogy: There are certain things my wife and I understand about each other that we could never have come to know apart from the love that makes each of us second nature to the other. Even so, we have reason to be confident about these things. As we have seen earlier, inside knowledge is not to be dismissed out of hand.

Moreover, the relationship between faith and reason works in both directions. Not only does reason come to the cleansing aid of faith, but faith enables reason to reach farther, to ask better questions, to become in every way more fully what it is meant to be. At least four good reasons can be given for this claim.

In the first place, revelation allows reason to work with greater confidence, because it provides us with additional grounds to believe that human intelligence is a gift of the divine intelligence, given to us for knowledge, rather than merely a haphazard, undependable hodgepodge that happened to come together in a process that was not planned.

In the second place, revelation provides certainty—at least relative certainty, because although God would be incapable of error, man could err in the interpretation of what God had disclosed—about points that are in principle within the scope of reason, but about which our reasoning might err.

In the third place, revelation provides new data, illuminating reality more deeply than reason could have done on its own. For example, there is the historical fact of the Fall, explaining why our hearts are so divided against themselves. And there is the promise that this interior dislocation in the core of our being can be cured.

Finally, revelation calls the mind's attention to a great many things that it *should* have been able to find out on its own, but may not have. Even in everyday experience we fail to notice things that should be obvious, like the fact that I am holding my "lost" glasses in my left hand. In the same way, we may be nearly blind to the facts of created reality until their Creator says, "Look here," and then we can see them. Consider for example the idea that human beings are *persons,* that they are not just *whats* but *whos.* This insight has transformed the West. Most people do not consider the notion of personhood particularly religious, yet it did not enter Western thought until the early controversies about the nature of the Trinity.

Of course, even granted that it may be reasonable to believe and assent to revelation, one must still take that step of believing and assenting. I am standing at an upper-floor window of a burning hotel. Someone calls to me from below:

"Jump! We'll catch you!"

"Who are you?" I cry.

"We're firemen. We have a net. Jump now!"

"But I can't see you. There's too much smoke."

"You don't have to see us. We can see *you.* Jump!"

"But I might break my neck. How can I believe you're who you say you are? How can I believe you will catch me?"

"Trust us. *Jump.*"

Though I may have every reason to believe that the unseen fire-fighters will catch me in their net, I may not trust them enough to overcome my fear, and so, hesitating, I may burn to death. Obviously, my reasons are not the same as trust; trust surpasses reason. Even so, my reasons are reasons *for* trust. So with religious faith: though it surpasses reason, it is not irrational.

Underlying the challenge, "What does faith have to do with reason?" is an assumption—usually unexamined—that faith and reason are at odds with each other. This supposition makes interesting bedfellows, for it is the one point that extreme secularists and extreme fundamentalists have in common. The former imagine that by rejecting faith they are choosing reason; the latter imagine that by rejecting reason they are choosing faith. Though it may come as a surprise to both groups, Christianity has historically rejected both of these views, holding that disciplined faith and disciplined reason are not enemies, but allies. John Paul II remarked that they are like the two wings of a bird, both of them necessary to fly.[2]

In fact, rejecting faith leads not to putting reason in place of faith, but to unreasonable faith. Consider, for example, the unofficial established religion of secular universities like the one where I teach. The university does not insist that there is no God. However, one is strongly expected to act as though if there were a God He could not make a difference to anything else, especially to one's scholarship. In other words, one is supposed to believe at most in an irrelevant God. Notice that this stance does not make the secular university neutral among religions. On the contrary, it puts it diametrically at odds with Christianity, for the Christian faith believes in a relevant God, Who does make a difference to everything, including scholarship, since He is the First Truth on which every other truth depends.

And there is more. If I consider God irrelevant, it does not follow that I do not worship any god at all. What follows is that I bow to different supreme concerns, different unconditional loyalties. Although such deities are not usually acknowledged, in effect I am worshipping gods other than God. Historically, Christianity has proposed reasons for trusting in the God that it professes and adores; it proposes a reasonable faith. But the intellectual culture of my secular university does not propose reasons for trusting in the gods to which it bends the knee—gods such as conformity, approval, recognition, status, power, self-importance, and self-will. It does not even know the knee is bent. In the name of reason, it pursues an unreasonable faith.

Christianity has delved more deeply into these matters than other religions because of its teaching that God Himself is interested in us and desires that we know Him. Joseph Cardinal Ratzinger wrote that in the early days of Christianity, "in an environment teeming with gods," when believers were asked to which god their God corresponded, "the answer ran: to none of them. To none of the gods to whom you pray but solely and alone to him to whom you do not pray, to that highest being of whom your philosophers speak." But there was a difference, for the philosophers who spoke of this highest being would never have dreamed of praying to him. By contrast, "[b]y deciding exclusively in favor of the God of the philosophers and logically declaring this God to be the God who speaks to man *and to whom one can pray*, the Christian faith gave a completely new significance to this God of the philosophers, removing him from the purely academic realm and thus transforming him." Ratzinger concludes, "this God of the philosophers, whose pure eternity and unchangeability had excluded any relation with the changeable and transitory, now appeared to the eye of faith as the God of men, who is not only thought of all thoughts, the eternal mathematics of the universe, but also *agape*, the power of creative love" [emphasis in the original].[3]

But don't thousands of religions claim divine revelation? Actually, most don't. For example, Siddhartha Gautama Buddha did not claim divine revelation; in fact, he seems to have denied that there are any divinities, and the Theravada branch of Buddhism continues this tradition. The Greeks did not claim divine revelation; they worshipped the gods of the poets, myths blending loveliness and horror, "gleams of celestial strength and beauty falling on a jungle of filth and imbecility."[4] Santería does not claim divine revelation; its rituals are a syncretic borrowing from a number of religions, with the aim of bargaining with the gods for power. Some contemporary religions, such as Wicca, are more or less consciously made up. Their practitioners do not claim that their teachings are revealed truths, but that they find these teachings pleasing and empowering.

In fact, just three major religions do claim divine revelation in historical rather than forgotten mythical time: Judaism, which Christianity considers its older brother; Christianity itself, which believes itself to be the fulfillment and extension of the promises God made to the Jews; and Islam, which relativizes both Jewish and Christian revelation, regards Jesus as just another prophet, and retreats to a more primitive understanding of God. This puts Christianity in a special position.

Christianity claims that information exceeding everything that human reason can discover—but with keen bearing on the reasonable questions we have been pursuing in this book—has actually been disclosed by God Himself, in historical time. This chapter has not "proven" the claim. I hope it has shown that it is reasonable.

In fact, it seems that by the light of revelation, the mind is able not only to see more clearly those things that lie within its natural reach, but also to understand and explain many other features of the world that would otherwise have remained utterly baffling. If this is true, then when reason rejects revelation, it is not being more true to itself, but less. Only illuminated by God can it come into its own.

The hope of the faith is that one day our thoughts may be lit not only by the reflected light of revelation, but by the direct illumination of the face of God Himself: that although now our minds only smolder, one day they will blaze like suns.

# CHAPTER 25

# The Paradoxes of Perfect Fulfillment

"Life is not an illogicality; yet it is a trap for logicians."[1]

Happiness is paradoxical. I don't mean that the idea of happiness is absurd or self-contradictory; a paradox is something that at first glance may seem absurd or self-contradictory but isn't. The topic of happiness is full of such paradoxes.

We encountered several of them in the very first chapter above—oddities about happiness that present such a stumbling block that some people throw up their hands and say we shouldn't pursue happiness at all. Recall, for instance, the paradox that those who are always asking, "How can I be happy?" are the very ones least likely to be happy. This is quite true, but why is it true? Because obsession with my happiness focuses my attention on myself, but my happiness lies in something outside myself, in the vision of God in His own being. To be fulfilled, I must stop worrying about my fulfillment—yet I must pursue and desire *that in which* my fulfillment lies, which is God. No doubt, when I begin to pursue God, my focus is on my own fulfillment in Him. Yet fulfillment in Him comes not because I think more and more about my fulfillment, but because I think less and less about my fulfillment and more and more about Him. So when the tradition declares that a man must lose himself to find himself,[2] there could hardly be a greater paradox, and yet there could hardly be a greater literal truth.

I don't expect this fact to be obvious from outside the experience itself. But it shouldn't be altogether obscure either, because so many things about even earthly loves bear the stamp of the paradox that you must lose yourself to find himself. Consider marriage. My wife and I are immensely enriched by our care for each other. But how can we be? How can it be wonderful to have someone else to worry about, twice the care? Yet it is. I would die for her—how can that make sense? But not to do so if she were in danger would be a greater death to me than death would be.

Or consider having children. Offspring convert us; they force us to become different beings. They plunge into our lives, filling their diapers, consuming time and attention, using up disposable income, upsetting all our comfortable arrangements, and nobody knows how they will turn out. Many couples decline to have any children at all, preferring what is sometimes called the "childfree" lifestyle because it leaves them more at liberty to do what they like. A puzzled writer who stops barely short of condemning all childbearing says neverthe-less, "I don't have the answer to the origin of the longing for children that many experience. It's almost certainly due to a complex mixture of biological and social factors. It might even be an *evolutionary trick*" [emphasis added].[3] Oh happy trick, that won for us so glorious a blessing! Willy-nilly, children knock us out of our complacent hab-its and force us to live outside ourselves; they are the necessary and natural continuation of that shock to our egotism which is initiated by marriage itself, and we are the better for it.

So perhaps it is not inconceivable that to find ourselves we must lose ourselves. I cannot urge strongly enough that this is best done with others. We saw earlier that even the most perfect earthly love always leaves something to be desired. But what better use of earthly love could there be than for friends or lovers to walk *together* into that divine mystery which is so much greater than themselves?

Supreme happiness presents other paradoxes too. One of them is that suffering and unhappiness in this life can conform us more closely to the God in whom our ultimate happiness lies. I don't mean that suffering becomes comfortable, or that unhappiness becomes sweet. But if the Atonement really happened—if it is really true that the Son of God entered into our suffering and took the worst of it upon Himself—then the face of pain changes. It would be impossible to offer our sorrow and heartache to a God who had never known pain. But if He has suffered for our sake, then we can offer our affliction to be joined, by His favor, with His own, so that it will prepare us more deeply to see Him. There is no way to prove this from the outside, but centuries of the experience of faith testify to its truth.

From this truth emerges another surprise. We saw earlier in this book that the fragmentary and incomplete happiness of the present life lies in the exercise of the virtues—along with a certain amount of good fortune, for otherwise the virtues have nothing on which to operate. But consider: If the deficiencies of good fortune—even suffering—can be turned by God's grace to our advantage, then doesn't this fact have implications not just for the perfect and complete happiness of seeing God, but even for fragmentary and incomplete happiness in the present life?

The continuation of this paradox is another: In some sense God sees to the needs of those who trust Him—though the idea is ridiculous if taken in the sense of a well-known pop song:

> Oh Lord, won't you buy me a Mercedes Benz
> My friends all drive Porsches, I must make amends.[4]

Yet there is a very great advantage in not having too much of the ordinary blessings of this life, because then we are set free from the temptation to place our confidence in these blessings instead of in God. The tradition does not say that God is near to the well off and saves the exalted in spirit; it says He is "near to the brokenhearted, and saves the crushed in spirit."[5] Jesus goes so far as to tell the poor that they are "blessed," that is, supremely happy.[6] The point is not that supreme happiness lies in sickness, starvation, and homelessness, but that it lies in supreme reliance on God, an attitude rarely to be found among those who have (for the moment) everything that this world offers.

But speaking of the ordinary blessings of life, doesn't Christ promise, "But seek first his kingdom and his righteousness, and all these things shall be yours as well"?[7] Obviously there is no guarantee that every one of His followers will always have enough to pay the rent. But without dismissing the literal meaning of his expression "all these things," we should notice that there is another way of taking it, too. Addressing God Himself, Augustine wrote:

> Ambition seeks honor and glory, although You alone are to be honored before all and glorious forever. By cruelty the great seek to be feared, yet who is to be feared but God alone: from His power what can be wrested away, or when or where or how or by whom? The caresses by which the lustful seduce are a seeking for love: but nothing is more caressing than Your charity, nor is anything more healthfully loved than Your supremely lovely, supremely luminous Truth. Curiosity may be regarded as a desire for

knowledge, whereas You supremely know all things. Ignorance and sheer stupidity hide under the names of simplicity and innocence: yet no being has simplicity like to Yours:
and none is more innocent than You, for it is their own
deeds that harm the wicked. Sloth pretends that it wants
quietude: but what sure rest is there save the Lord? Luxu-
riousness would be called abundance and completeness;
but You are the fullness and inexhaustible abundance of
incorruptible delight. Wastefulness is a parody of generosity: but You are the infinitely generous giver of all good.
Avarice wants to possess overmuch: but You possess all.
Enviousness claims that it strives to excel: but what can
excel before You? Anger clamors for just vengeance: but
whose vengeance is so just as Yours? Fear is the recoil from
a new and sudden threat to something one holds dear, and
a cautious regard for one's own safety: but nothing new or
sudden can happen to You, nothing can threaten Your
hold upon things loved, and where is safety secure save in
You? Grief pines at the loss of things in which desire
delighted: for it wills to be like to You from whom nothing
can be taken away....

Augustine's argument is that the only possible sense in which we
can "have everything" is to have God; all of the created goods we
desire are but pale reflections of the uncreated Good that is Himself.
In a twisted way, even those blown by the storms of greed and craving are trying to be like Him who is all-sufficient. "Thus even those
who go from You and stand up against You are still perversely imitat-
ing You. But by the mere fact of their imitation, they declare that You
are the creator of all that is, and that there is nowhere for them to go
where You are not."[8]

I have mentioned the paradoxical beatitude, "Blessed are the poor," but all of the Beatitudes—all of Christ's maxims about supreme happiness—are paradoxical. The mourners, the meek, those who hunger and thirst for righteousness, even the persecuted are called "blessed" or supremely happy.[9] These maxims are often misunderstood, I think. They are not commands, but declarations of how things are. Consider the mysterious saying, "Blessed are the pure of heart, for they shall see God."[10] We can view this from several perspectives.

First, we can view it as providing answers to a set of questions. Who will be supremely happy? The sort of persons who are pure in heart. What is their delight? Seeing God. Why are they so delighted to see Him? Because by His grace working in them, they have become the kind of people who do long to see Him, for that is what a pure heart is. To those whose hearts are pure enough to long for Him, God promises satisfaction—and because they trust in His promise, they already have that foretaste of happiness which is hope, even though in this life they do not yet have fulfillment.

Second, we can view it as the solution to a riddle. Seeing God is the complete and consummate good of everyone, but not everyone wants it; we may prefer happiness to be what we want it to be rather than what it is. God does not promise consummation to everyone who wants to be happy. He promises it to those who desire above all to have *what happiness really is,* which is Himself, and who cooperate with the grace by which He gives it. To them He gives such great goods, such incredibly wonderful blessings, that we would tremble to conceive them. But until we are right in our hearts, we cannot even recognize them as good.

Thus, Christ is not saying that the pure of heart are supremely happy because they get the hearts' desire of people with mixed motives and sullied hearts, like me. Rather He is saying that they are supremely happy because they get the hearts' desire of people whose hearts are pure. I must become that kind of person. I must give Him His way with me. I must allow Him to scour my heart and polish it until it can reflect His own light. I will, in the end, receive the object of my uttermost longing, but only if my uttermost longing is for the one thing that can satisfy it.

At last we come to the final paradox of perfect happiness, which is our present unfulfillment. *Not yet being fulfilled* is a sign not of something wrong but of accurate perception, for we are not fulfilled here, and it is not the pretense of premature fulfillment that makes us happy. An ancient prayer refers to us as "mourning and weeping in this vale of tears." St. Paul spoke searchingly of how we "groan" in the longing that what is mortal in us may be "swallowed up by life."[11] These very tears and groaning are promissory notes of joy, for if we were perfectly adapted to the way of the world, we would not have such tears and groanings; the ordinary satisfactions would satisfy us. I weep, therefore I rejoice.

Blessed are those who refuse to drug their discontent with futile satisfactions. Supremely happy are those who settle for nothing less than supreme happiness.

# Acknowledgements

I am a fairly solitary worker. Most of the help I receive is simply encouragement from friends, well-wishers, and readers. That is true meat and true drink. After one writes a number of books, one finds oneself acknowledging the same people over and over, because the same people are so generous over and over. Since I have thanked them before, and since I may not have many books left in me, I think perhaps my friends will not mind if this time I do something different.

One of the things one learns, if he lives long enough, is that he is a debtor to a great many people whose benefactions he never knew at the time. And so I here offer my heartfelt thanks and acknowledgement to all those souls whom I cannot name, who at one time or another saw fit to plead my cause to God—or sometimes to man. At times without number, especially in the early years, this petition must have seemed a lost cause. I am more grateful for these undeserved mercies than I could tell in a hundred lifetimes, and the weight of my debt burns like glory.

# Notes

## Dedication
Proverbs 31:26 (King James Version, hereinafter cited as KJV).

## Preface
1.  Anicius Manlius Severinus Boethius, *The Consolation of Philosophy*, trans. H. R. James (1897), book 3, chapter 2, prose section.
2.  The *Treatise* comprises the first five questions of the first part of the second part of Thomas Aquinas's *Summa Theologiae*.
3.  J. Budziszewski, *Commentary on Thomas Aquinas's Treatise on Happiness and Ultimate Purpose* (Cambridge: Cambridge University Press, 2020).
4.  Aristotle, *Nicomachean Ethics*, trans. W. D. Ross (1925), book 2, chapter 5.
5.  In chapter 13 below from J. Budziszewski, *On the Meaning of Sex* (Wilmington, Delaware: Intercollegiate Studies Institute, 2012); in chapter 20 and 24 from J. Budziszewski, *Commentary on Thomas Aquinas's Treatise on Law* (Cambridge: Cambridge University Press, 2014); in chapter 24 from J. Budziszewski, *Commentary on Thomas Aquinas's Treatise on Divine Law* (Cambridge: Cambridge University Press, 2021); and in chapter 25, from Budziszewski, *Commentary on Thomas Aquinas's Treatise on Happiness*.

## Part One: Getting Started
1.  Blaise Pascal, *Thoughts*, trans. O. W. Wight (1910), book 1, chapter 1. Pascal was speaking of man himself; I have applied the description to man's opinions of happiness.

## Chapter 1: Why Is How to Be Happy or Fulfilled Even a Question?
1.  Plato, *Meno*, in *Laches, Protagoras, Meno, Euthydemus*, trans. W. R. M. Lamb (Cambridge, Massachusetts: Harvard University Press, 1952), 297, 299. Meno

is admitting that he doesn't know what virtue is; I have applied the remark to happiness.

2. Alexandra Sifferlin, "Here's How Happy Americans Are Right Now," *Time*, July 26, 2017, https://time.com/4871720/how-happy-are-americans.

3. Justin McCarthy, "New High of 90% of Americans Satisfied with Personal Life," Gallup, February 6, 2020, https://news.gallup.com/poll/284285/new-high-americans-satisfied-personal-life.aspx.

4. Aristotle, *Nicomachean Ethics*, book 1, chapter 4.

5. Rafael Euba, "Humans Aren't Designed to Be Happy—So Stop Trying," The Conversation, July 19, 2019, https://theconversation.com/humans-arent-designed-to-be-happy-so-stop-trying-119262.

### Chapter 2: How Not to Find the Answer to the Question—and How to Find It

1. Aristotle, *Nicomachean Ethics*, trans. W. D. Ross (1925), book 1, chapter 2.

2. F. Y. Edgeworth, *Mathematical Psychics* (1881), especially chapter 3, "On Hedonimetry."

3. Mortimer J. Adler, *The Time of Our Lives: The Ethics of Common Sense* (New York: Fordham University Press, 1996).

4. Thomas Aquinas, *Summa Theologiae*, trans. Fathers of the English Dominican Province (1920), first part of the second part, question 32, article 3, reply to objection 3.

5. I consider the possibility of a reasonable but *non*-ordinary source of data very close to the end of the book, but I do not want to bring it in until it is strictly necessary to do so.

### Chapter 3: What We All Mean by Happiness—Whatever It Is

1. F. Scott Fitzgerald, *The Beautiful and Damned* (1922), book 3, chapter 1.

2. Bud Abbott and Lou Costello, "Who's on First?" radio routine from the 1930s, http://www.baseball-almanac.com/humor4.shtml. The original author is disputed.

3. Aristotle, *Metaphysics*, trans. W. D. Ross (1924), book 4, chapter 2.

4. William Shakespeare, *Henry V*, act 4, scene 3, lines 58–67.

5. Aristotle, *Nicomachean Ethics*, book 1, chapter 4.

### Part Two: Getting On with It

1. Plato, *Republic*, trans. Benjamin Jowett (1892), book 4.

## Chapter 4: Could Wealth Be Happiness?

1. Charles Dickens, *David Copperfield* (1850), chapter 12.
2. Steve Siebold, *How Rich People Think* (Park Ridge, Illinois: London House, 2010). The first quotation is from the jacket flap. The three adages are the titles of chapters 3, 4, and 9, respectively.
3. "But seek ye first the kingdom of God, and his righteousness; and all these things shall be added unto you." Matthew 6:33 (KJV).
4. Alasdair MacIntyre, *After Virtue*, 2nd ed. (Notre Dame, Indiana: University of Notre Dame Press, 1984).
5. "From 1999 through 2018, the age-adjusted suicide rate increased 35%." Holly Hedegaard, Sally C. Curtin, and Margaret Warner, "Increase in Suicide Mortality in the United States, 1999–2018," NCHS data brief, no. 362, National Center for Health Statistics, 2020.
6. Mary C. Daly, Daniel J. Wilson, and Norman J. Johnson, "Relative Status and Well-Being: Evidence from U.S. Suicide Deaths," Federal Reserve Bank of San Francisco Working Paper Series, September 2012, https://www.frbsf.org/economic-research/files/wp12-16bk.pdf. The authors show that the difference cannot be explained by variations in the cost of living, in access to emergency medical care, or in how suicides are counted.
7. Judith Warner, *And Then They Stopped Talking to Me: Making Sense of Middle School* (New York: Crown, 2020), 161.
8. Jonathan Swift, "The Battle of the Books" (1704), Project Gutenberg, January 15, 2007, http://www.gutenberg.org/files/623/623-h/623-h.htm.
9. Joseph Addison, *The Spectator*, no. 256, December 24, 1711, Project Gutenberg, http://www.gutenberg.org/files/12030/12030-h/12030-h/SV2/Spectator2.html.
10. Economists use the expression "expected value" for the magnitude of a gain or loss multiplied by its probability. It is safe to say that if the expected value of losing something is greater than the sheer enjoyment of having it, then the person who has it is a net loser—even in terms of mere pleasure.
11. Anicius Manlius Severinus Boethius, *The Consolation of Philosophy*, trans. H. R. James, (1897), book 2.
12. John Donne, *Devotions upon Emergent Occasions* (1624), meditation 17.
13. Dorothy Day, "Decent Poverty the Social Ideal," in *American Catholic Thought on Social Questions*, ed. Aaron I. Abell (Indianapolis, Indiana: Bobbs-Merrill, 1968).

## Chapter 5: Could Bodily Health or Beauty Be Happiness?

1. Harriet Prescott Spofford, *Evanescence* (1911).

2.  "U.S. National Health Expenditure as percent of GDP from 1960 to 2020," Statista, 2021, https://www.statista.com/statistics/184968/us-health-expenditure-as-percent-of-gdp-since-1960. In 2019, 17.8 percent of GDP and rising: roughly one out of every five and a half dollars.

3.  Sometimes called "positive body image" or "body positivity," this is related to the topic of Chapter 8, "Could Loving or Esteeming Ourselves Be Happiness?"

4.  For example, the market for men's skincare products grew by 8 percent in 2019. "Men's Skincare Products Market—an Emerging Disruptor In Beauty Industry," *Beauty Business Journal*, November 25, 2019, https://beautybusinessjournal.com/mens-skincare-products-market-an-emerging-disruptor-in-beauty-industry.

5.  Psalm 139:14 (KJV).

6.  Kara Babcock, review of Max Barry, *Machine Man*, Goodreads, August 7, 2011, https://www.goodreads.com/book/show/6634696-machine-man.

7.  Augusten Burroughs, *Dry: A Memoir*, 2nd ed. (New York: Macmillan, 2013), 286.

8.  Arthur Schopenhauer, *The Essays of Arthur Schopenhauer: The Wisdom of Life*, trans. T. Bailey Saunders, chapter 2, Project Gutenberg, https://www.gutenberg.org/files/10741/10741-h/10741-h.htm.

9.  This conversation is part of "The Meaning of Sexual Beauty," chapter 6, in J. Budziszewski, *On the Meaning of Sex* (Wilmington, Delaware: ISI Books, 2012). Here I am not addressing the meaning of sexual beauty, but only the question of its relation to happiness.

10. This is why Christians look forward to the resurrection of the body, but I am not inquiring into that possibility at present.

## Chapter 6: Could Fame or Sheer Notice Be Happiness?

1.  Aulus Persius Flaccus, *Satires*, satire 1, line 28.

2.  Niccolo Machiavelli, *Discourses on the First Decade of Titus Livius*, trans. Ninian Hill Thomson (1883), chapters 26–27, Project Gutenberg, http://www.gutenberg.org/cache/epub/10827/pg10827.html.

3.  Joseph Addison, *The Spectator*, no. 255, December 22, 1711, Project Gutenberg, http://www.gutenberg.org/files/12030/12030-h/12030-h/SV2/Spectator2.html.

4.  Jon Deak, "Laughing Chewbacca Mask Lady (Full Video)," YouTube, May 19, 2016, https://www.youtube.com/watch?v=y3yRv5Jg5TI.

5.  The Late Late Show with James Corden, "Chewbacca Mom Gets Surprise from the Real Chewbacca," YouTube, May 24, 2016, https://www.youtube.com/watch?v=OT3MVRvoTT4.

6. Optimus Primal (@BlindDensetsu), "What kinda psychopathic behavior…," Twitter, June 29, 2019, 9:02 a.m., https://twitter.com/BlindDensetsu/status/1144954255318671366. The video itself has now been removed.

7. Grace Hauck, "Viral Blue Bell Saga Continues: Third Ice Cream Licker Arrested in Texas," *USA Today*, August 23, 2019, https://www.usatoday.com/story/news/nation/2019/08/23/blue-bell-ice-cream-licker-arrested-after-port-arthur-walmart-incident/2093855001. Indeed, licking things seems to be the moment's favored attention-getter. More recently a young "social influencer" was interviewed on a television news show after she posted a video (now removed) of herself licking a commercial airplane toilet seat. She too was honored by copycats.

8. Madringking 1119, "Leave Britney Alone (Complete)," YouTube, August 11, 2011, https://www.youtube.com/watch?v=WqSTXuJeTks. This video has been viewed over five million times.

## Chapter 7: Could Glory or Praise Be Happiness?

1. Publius Cornelius Tacitus, *Histories*, trans. Alfred John Church and William Jackson Brodribb (1864), book 4.

2. Augustine of Hippo, *The City of God against the Pagans*, trans. Marcus Dods (1887), book 5, chapter 12, www.newadvent.org/fathers.

3. Hamilton says "fame," but he is using that term for what we have been calling "glory" rather than mere notoriety.

4. Alexander Hamilton, *The Federalist*, no. 72.

5. "Esse quam videri bonus malebat: ita, quo minus petebat gloriam, eo magis illum sequebatur." Sallust (Gaius Sallustius Cripus), *The War Against Catiline*, book 54, chapter 6.

6. Augustine, *City of God*, book 5, chapters 12-21.

7. Joseph Addison, *The Spectator*, no. 257, December 25, 1711, Project Gutenberg, http://www.gutenberg.org/files/12030/12030-h/12030-h/SV2/Spectator2.html.

8. Augustine, *City of God*, book 5, chapter 12.

9. Ibid., chapter 22. Marcus Tullius Cicero exhibits this inconsistency in *On Duties*.

10. Joseph Addison, *The Spectator*, no. 255, December 22, 1711, Project Gutenberg, http://www.gutenberg.org/files/12030/12030-h/12030-h/SV2/Spectator2.html.

11. Jonathan Swift, *Thoughts on Various Subjects, Moral and Diverting* (1726).

12. Joseph Addison, *The Spectator*, no. 256, December 24, 1711, Project Gutenberg, http://www.gutenberg.org/files/12030/12030-h/12030-h/SV2/Spectator2.html.

13. Ibid.

## Chapter 8: Could Loving or Esteeming Ourselves Be Happiness?

1. John Milton, *Paradise Lost*, book 4, lines 460–62. Eve is dazzled by admiration of her own reflection in the water.

2. The expression "the virtue of selfishness" is associated with Ayn Rand and also with Nathaniel Branden, who along with various leftists and New Agers, was in at the Californian beginning of the self-esteem movement. See Ayn Rand and Nathaniel Branden, *The Virtue of Selfishness: A New Concept of Egoism* (New York: Signet, 1964).

3. The latter hope was "predicated on the observation that people with high self-regard earn more than others and therefore pay more in taxes." Roy F. Baumeister, "The Lowdown on High Self-Esteem: Thinking You're Hot Stuff Isn't the Promised Cure-All," *Los Angeles Times*, January 25, 2005, https://www.latimes.com/archives/la-xpm-2005-jan-25-oe-baumeister25-story.html.

4. Roy F. Baumeister, "Should Schools Try to Boost Self Esteem? Beware the Dark Side," *American Educator* 20, no. 2 (Summer 1996): 14–19, 43.

5. John Rosemond, *Family Building: The Five Fundamentals of Effective Parenting* (Kansas City, Missouri: Andrews McMeel, 2005), chapter 5.

6. Jean M. Twenge, *Generation Me: Why Today's Young Americans Are More Confident, Assertive, Entitled—and More Miserable Than Ever Before*, revised and updated (New York: Atria, 2006, 2014), 73.

7. Diane Loomans, *The Lovables in the Kingdom of Self-Esteem* (Belvedere Tiburon, California: H J Kramer, 1991).

8. Jamie Lee Curtis, *I'm Gonna Like Me: Letting Off a Little Self-Esteem* (New York: HarperCollins, 2002).

9. Emily Winfield Martin, *The Wonderful Things You Will Be* (New York: Random House Children's Books, 2015).

10. Luke 2:52 (KJV).

11. See Craig Malkin, *Rethinking Narcissism: The Secret to Recognizing and Coping with Narcissists* (New York: HarperWave, 2015) and C. Sedikides, E. A. Rudich, A. P. Gregg, M. Kumashiro, and C. Rusbult, "Are Normal Narcissists Psychologically Healthy?: Self-Esteem Matters," *Journal of Personality and Social Psychology* 87, no. 3 (2004): 400–16, https://doi.org/10.1037/0022-3514.87.3.400.

12. Baumeister, "The Lowdown on High Self-Esteem."

13. Donelson R. Forsyth, Natalie K. Lawrence, Jeni L. Burnette, and Roy F. Baumeister, "Attempting to Improve the Academic Performance of Struggling College Students by Bolstering Their Self–Esteem: An Intervention that Backfired," *Journal of Social and Clinical Psychology* 26, no. 4 (2007): 447–59.

14. Delroy L. Paulhus, "Interpersonal and Intrapsychic Adaptiveness of Trait Self-Enhancement: A Mixed Blessing?" *Journal of Personality and Social Psychology* 74, no. 5 (1998): 1197–1208.

15. Roy F. Baumeister and John Tierney, *Willpower: Rediscovering the Greatest Human Strength* (New York: Penguin, 2011), 193.

16. For some of these trends, see Twenge, *Generation Me*.

17. Whitney Houston, "Greatest Love of All," *Whitney Houston*, Arista Records, 1985, written by Michael Masser and Linda Creed.

18. Meghan Trainor, "I Love Me," *Thank You*, Apple Music / Epic Records, 2016, written by Meghan Trainor, Eric Frederic, Jacob Kasher Hindlin, Gamal Lewis, and Thomas Troelsen.

19. Sia, "The Greatest," *The Greatest*, Monkey Puzzle / RCA, 2016, written by Greg Kurstin, Kendrick Lamar, Blair Mackichan, and Sia Kate Furler.

20. Rivers Cuomo, "The Greatest Man That Ever Lived," *Weezer*, DGC and Interscope Records, 2008, written by Rivers Cuomo. The choice of metaphor is interesting, since radioactivity kills.

21. Meghan Trainor, "Me Too," *Thank You*, Apple Music / Epic Records, 2016, written by Meghan Trainor, Eric Frederic, Jacob Kasher Hindlin, Jason Desrouleaux, and Peter Svensson.

22. Ally Brooke, "Fabulous," Latium LLC / Atlantic Records, 2020, written by Alley Brooke Hernandez.

23. Christina Aguilera, "Beautiful," *Stripped*, RCA / Sony, 2002, written by Linda Perry.

24. India Arie, "Video," *Acoustic Soul*, Motown, 2001, written by India Arie, Carlos "6 July" Broady, and Shannon Sanders.

25. Lady Gaga, "Born This Way," *Born This Way*, Abbey Road / Germano, 2011, written by Stefani Germanotta (Lady Gaga) and Jeppe Laursen.

26. Alessia Cara, "Okay Okay," *This Summer*, Def Jam / Universal Music Canada, 2019, written by Alessia Caracciolo (Cara) and Jon Levine.

27. Leviticus 19:18; Matthew 22:39. The wording is almost identical across translations.

28. Thomas Aquinas, *Summa Theologiae*, trans. Fathers of the English Dominican Province (1920), second part of the second part, question 44, article 7.

## Chapter 9: Could Power or Responsibility Be Happiness?

1. Thomas Hobbes, *Leviathan* (1651), part 1, chapter 11. I have modernized the spelling in this quotation.

2. Ibid., chapter 10.

3. Josiah Gilbert Holland, *History of Western Massachusetts* (1855), chapter 18, p. 296. Shays' Rebellion took place in 1786–1787.

4. Anicius Manlius Severinus Boethius, *The Consolation of Philosophy*, trans. H. R. James (1897), book 3, chapter 5, prose section. I have modernized the language in this quotation.

5. Marcus Annaeus Lucanus (Lucan), *Pharsalia*, trans. A. S. Kline (2014), book 1, line 92, https://www.poetryintranslation.com/PITBR/Latin/PharsaliaImaster.php#anchor_Toc390000073.

6. John Emerich Edward Dalberg-Acton, "Letter to Bishop Mandell Creighton," April 5, 1887, in John Emerich Edward Dalberg-Acton, *Historical Essays and Studies*, ed. John Neville Figgis and Reginald Vere Laurence (London: Macmillan, 1907).

7. Believed to be Robert Yates, a New York judge.

8. Brutus (Robert Yates), "Letter 4," in Herbert J. Storing with Murray Dry, eds., *The Anti-Federalist* (Chicago: University of Chicago Press, 1985). The story is biblical; it can be found in 2 Kings 8.

9. Lucius Annaeus Seneca the Younger, *Moral Letters to Lucilius*, letter 90, section 34.

10. David Hume, *A Treatise of Human Nature*, book 2, chapter 3, section 3.

11. Lucius Annaeus Seneca the Younger, *Phaedra*, in John G. Fitch, *Tragedies: Volume 1*, Loeb Classical Library, vol. 62 (Cambridge, Massachusetts: Harvard University Press, 2002), line 215, p. 435.

## Chapter 10: Could Pleasure or Delight Be Happiness?

1. Inscription over the gate to the garden of the philosopher Epicurus, as quoted in Lucius Annaeus Seneca, *Selected Letters*, trans. Elaine Fantham (Oxford: Oxford University Press, 2010), letter 21, section 10, p. 39.

2. Black Eyed Peas, "I Gotta Feeling," *The E.N.D.*, Square Prod / Metropolis Studios, 2009, written by William Adams, Stacy Ferguson, Jamie Gomez, David Guetta, Allan Pineda, and Frédéric Riesterer.

3. Thomas Aquinas, *Summa Theologiae*, trans. Fathers of the English Dominican Province (1920), second part of the second part, question 168, article 2.

4. C. S. Lewis, *That Hideous Strength: A Modern Fairy-Tale for Grown-Ups* (London: Bodley Head, 1945), chapter 12. Lewis was not commenting on pornography in particular, but explaining the force of perverse and unnatural attractions in general.

5. Dante Alighieri, *Inferno* (third part of the *Divine Comedy*), trans. Anthony Esolen (New York: Modern Library, 2002), canto 29, lines 75–80. Alchemists

are punished in hell because they falsify things, just as impostors falsify persons, counterfeiters falsify money, and perjurers falsify words.

6. Positive psychologist Martin E. P. Seligman, for example, says that the first pillar of positive psychology is the study of positive emotion. See Seligman's foreword in *Flourishing: Positive Psychology and the Life Well-Lived*, by Corey L. M. Keyes and Jonathan Haidt, eds., (Washington, D.C.: American Psychological Association, 2003), xii; cf. xvi.

## Chapter 11: *Could Painlessness or Annihilation Be Happiness?*
1. Herman Melville, *Moby Dick*, chapter 42.
2. Aristotle, *Nicomachean Ethics*, trans. W. D. Ross (1925), book 1.
3. Horace Smith, *Qui Bono?* (a burlesque of his contemporary, Lord Byron), lines 71–72.
4. Thomas Nagel, "The Absurd," *Journal of Philosophy* 68, no. 20 (1971): 716–27.
5. "This is the most beautiful thing I've ever read….," Reddit, 2014, https://www.reddit.com/r/philosophy/comments/2ws4lo/this_is_the_most_beautiful_thing_ive_ever_read_if/.

## Chapter 12: *Could Meaning or Commitment Be Happiness?*
1. Viktor Frankl, preface to *Man's Search for Meaning* (Boston: Beacon Press, 1992).
2. *Alcoholics Anonymous*, 4th ed. (Alcoholics Anonymous World Services, Inc., 2001), 59.
3. Jonathan Haidt, *The Happiness Hypothesis* (New York: Basic Books, 2006), 193. Haidt is alluding to a statement in Mircea Eliade, *The Sacred and the Profane: The Nature of Religion*, trans. W. R. Task (San Diego, California: Harcourt Brace, 1959), 24.
4. Ibid., 193–94.
5. Ibid., 196.
6. Ibid., 195–96.
7. Christopher Peterson and Martin E. P. Seligman, *Character Strengths and Virtues: A Handbook and Classification* (Oxford: Oxford University Press, 2004), 34.
8. Martin E. P. Seligman, *Flourish: A Visionary New Understanding of Happiness and Well-Being* (New York: Free Press, 2011), 261–62.
9. Aristotle, *Nicomachean Ethics*, book 1, chapter 10.

## Chapter 13: Could Love or Friendship Be Happiness?

1. Augustine of Hippo, *Confessions*, trans. Frank J. Sheed (Indianapolis: Hackett, 2006), book 4, chapter 6. Augustine is alluding to Horace, *Carmina*, book 1, ode 3, line 8.
2. 2 Samuel 1:26 (New American Bible).
3. The distinction is from Thomas Aquinas. For further discussion see J. Budizewszki, "Thomas Aquinas on Marriage, Fruitfulness, and Faithful Love," in Theresa Notare, ed., *Humanae Vitae 50 Years Later: A Compendium* (Washington, D.C.: Catholic University of America Press, 2019).
4. Aristotle, *Nicomachean Ethics*, trans. W. D. Ross (1925), book 9, chapter 4.
5. Song of Songs 8:6 (Revised Standard Version Catholic Edition, hereinafter RSV-CE).
6. Song of Songs 3:5 (RSV-CE).

## Chapter 14: Could Virtue Be Happiness?

1. Alexander Pope, *Essay on Man*, epistle 4, line 309.
2. Lucius Annaeus Seneca the Younger, *On Benefits*, trans. Aubrey Stewart (1887), book 4, chapter 12.
3. Benedictus de Spinoza, *Ethics*, part 5, proposition 42, trans. Robert Harvey Monro Elwes (1670; trans. 1887).
4. Plato, *Gorgias*, trans. Benjamin Jowett (1892).
5. Marcus Tullius Cicero, *Tusculan Disputations*, trans. J. E. King (1927), book 5, chapter 25, section 72, and chapter 26, section 73, Stoic Therapy, https://www.stoictherapy.com/elibrary-tusculan-king#book5.
6. Marcus Tullius Cicero, "A Man Who Is Virtuous Is Destitute of No Requisite of a Happy Life," *Stoic Paradoxes*, paradox 2, in *Three Books of Offices or Moral Duties*, trans. C. R. Edmonds (1855), Stoic Therapy, https://www.stoictherapy.com/elibrary-stoicparadoxes#2. I have paraphrased this and some other translations in this chapter to avoid awkwardness and archaism.
7. Aristotle, *Nicomachean Ethics*, trans. W. D. Ross (1925), book 7, chapter 13.
8. Of course the two questions are connected, but we can put off exploring their relationship until later.
9. Marcus Aurelius Antoninus, *Meditations*, trans. George Long (1889), book 4, chapter 7, and book 8, chapter 47, The Internet Classics Archive, http://classics.mit.edu/Antoninus/meditations.html.
10. Cicero, *Stoic Paradoxes*, paradox 2.

11. Epictetus, *Discourses*, trans. George Long (1904), book 4, chapter 5. *The Discourses* are available at http://classics.mit.edu/Epictetus/discourses.mb.txt, from which subsequent quotations are also taken.

12. Ibid., book 3, chapter 13.

13. Cicero, *Tusculan Disputations*, book 5, chapter 18.

14. Cicero, *On the Ends of Goods and Evils*, trans. Harris Rackham (1914), book 4, chapter 28, section 78, University of Chicago, http://penelope.uchicago.edu/Thayer/E/Roman/Texts/Cicero/de_Finibus/home.html. Here the translator uses the phrase "Moral Worth." Cicero, however, refers to the *honestum*, which is the honest and honorable, taking the honest in the double sense of truthfulness and good faith, and taking the honorable in the double sense of receiving honor and being worthy to receive it. In view of the context, I render the term simply "virtue."

15. Ibid., book 4, chapter 26, section 72.

16. The other three Stoic justifications for suicide are complying with duty (for example, obeying a command of the oracle at Delphi), evading tyrants who would coerce us to do or shameful things, and finding a way out from dementia. See the fragment from Chrysippus in Margaret Pabst Battin, ed., *The Ethics of Suicide: Historical Sources* (Oxford: Oxford University Press, 2015), 91.

17. Epictetus, *Discourses*, book 1, chapter 25.

18. Ibid., chapter 24.

19. Decius speaking to his fellow citizens in Silius Italicus, *Punica*, trans. James Duff (1927), book 1, section 11, ToposText, https://topostext.org/work/248.

20. Augustine of Hippo, *The City of God against the Pagans*, trans. Marcus Dods (1887), book 19, chapter 4, www.newadvent.org/fathers.

21. Aristotle, *Nicomachean Ethics*, book 2, chapter 6.

22. Cicero, *Tusculan Disputations*, book 5, chapter 6, sections 16–17.

23. Jonathan Swift, *Thoughts on Various Subjects, Moral and Diverting* (1726).

24. Latin *conversio*, Greek *metabolē*.

25. Lucius Mestrius Plutarchus (Plutarch), "On Common Conceptions Against the Stoics," in *Moralia*, trans. W. C. Hembold, essay 74, chapter 10, Stoic Therapy, https://www.stoictherapy.com/elibrary-moralessays. Although Plutarch is a critic, there is no reason to doubt that he is drawing these analogies from the Stoics themselves.

26. Lucius Annaeus Seneca the Younger, *On the Happy Life*, trans. James Ker, in *Hardship and Happiness* (Chicago: University of Chicago Press, 2014), chapter 17, section 3, p. 255. Though a few sentences later Seneca said he will live as he ought "as soon as I can," he plainly thought the time would never come.

## Chapter 15: Does It All Come Down to Luck?

1. George Strait, "Ace in the Hole," MCA, 1989, written by Dennis Adkins.
2. Marcus Tullius Cicero, *Tusculan Disputations*, trans. J. E. King (1927), book 5, chapter 1, section 2, Stoic Therapy, https://www.stoictherapy.com/elibrary-tusculan-king#book5. He wasn't suggesting that luck really is sovereign.
3. Frank Loesser, "Luck Be a Lady," *Guys and Dolls*, 1950.
4. Niccolò Machiavelli, *The Prince*, chapter 25.
5. Lucius Mestrius Plutarchus (Plutarch), "On Fortune," in *Moralia*, trans. Frank Cole Babbitt (1928), section 5, Perseus Digital Library, http://www.perseus.tufts.edu/hopper/text?doc=Perseus%3atext%3a2008.01.0165.
6. Cicero, *Tusculan Disputations*, book 5, chapter 1, section 3.
7. Jonathan Swift, *Thoughts on Various Subjects, Moral and Diverting* (1726).
8. If the events are independent, then the probability of something happening 10 times in a row is the tenth power of probability of its happening once. Since in our example the probability of the event happening once is 1 out of 2, the probability of its happening ten times in a row is 1 out of 2 to the tenth power, which is one out of 1024.
9. Jonathan Swift, *Thoughts on Various Subjects, Moral and Diverting* (1726).
10. Plutarch, "On the Fortune or the Virtue of Alexander," in *Moralia*, trans. Frank Cole Babbitt (1936), chapter 2, section 8, http://www.perseus.tufts.edu/hopper/text?doc=Perseus%3Atext%3A2008.01.0231%3Achapter%3D2%3Asection%3D8. Plutarch says much the same of Romulus: "Virtue made Romulus great, but Fortune watched over him until he became great." Plutarch, "On the Fortune of the Romans," in *Moralia*, trans. Frank Cole Babbit (1936), book 2, chapter 8, https://penelope.uchicago.edu/Thayer/e/roman/texts/plutarch/moralia/fortuna_romanorum*.html.
11. Lucius Annaeus Seneca the Younger, *Letters from a Stoic*, trans. Richard M. Gummere (1917), letter 13, section 11.
12. "Which, like the toad, ugly and venomous, wears yet a precious jewel in his head." William Shakespeare, *As You Like It*, act 2, scene 1, lines 14–16.
13. Francis de la Rochefoucauld, *Maxims*, trans. J. W. Willis Bund and J. Hain Friswell (1871), no. 25.
14. Aristotle, *Nicomachean Ethics*, trans. W. D. Ross (1925), book 7, chapter 13.
15. Proverbial expression based on the Parable of the Talents, Matthew 25:14–30.
16. Proverbs 9:1–4a (RSV-CE).
17. Such studies have other problems too. For example, statements like "character depends 65 percent on genes and 35 percent on environment" are misleading because they treat these two influences as though they were independent. They

aren't: Environment affects the expression of the genes, and genes affect response to the environment. Self-discipline affects both.

## Chapter 16: Could Anything in This World Be Happiness?

1. John 4:13 (New King James Version).
2. Whittaker Chambers, foreword to *Witness* (New York: Random House, 1952).
3. C. S. Lewis, preface to *The Pilgrim's Regress*, 3rd ed. (New York: Bantam Books, 1986), p. xii.
4. The poem, *Tegner's Drapa* (1849), was Henry Wadsworth Longfellow's translation of a death dirge by the Swedish poet Esaias Tegnér.
5. Henry Wadsworth Longfellow, "Day is Done" (1844).
6. Augustine of Hippo, *Writings of Saint Augustine*, trans. Mary Sarah Muldowney (New York: Fathers of the Church, Inc., 1947), vol. 38, sermon 241, section 2, p. 256. I have replaced the word "acknowledgment" with the word "confession," which more accurately reflects the original Latin *confessio*.

## Chapter 17: The Imperfect Happiness to Which These Reflections Point

1. Job 7:1a (RSV-CE).
2. Anicius Manlius Severinus Boethius, *The Consolation of Philosophy*, trans. H. R. James (1897), book 3, chapter 2, prose section, Lady Philosophy speaking.
3. Augustine of Hippo, *The City of God against the Pagans*, trans. Marcus Dods (1887), book 19, chapter 4, New Advent, www.newadvent.org/fathers.
4. Samuel Johnson, "The Requisites to True Friendship," *The Rambler*, no. 64, October 27, 1750.
5. Samuel Johnson, "Uncertainty of Friendship," *The Idler*, no. 23, September 23, 1758.

## Part Three: Starting Over

1. Plato, *Republic*, trans. Benjamin Jowett (1892), book 2.

## Chapter 18: Why Shouldn't We Settle for Imperfect Happiness?

1. Dante Alighieri, *Inferno* (third part of the *Divine Comedy*), trans. Anthony Esolen (New York: Modern Library, 2002), canto 4, lines 40–43.
2. A common saying.
3. Giacomo Samek Lodovici, "The Role of God in Aquinas' Ethical Thought: Can an Atheist Be Moral?," presented at the conference "Ethics Without God?" the

Jacques Maritain Center, Notre Dame University, July 2003, https://maritain.nd.edu/jmc/ti03/eSamek.htm.

4. Ecclesiastes 12:12 (RSV-CE).

5. William James, "The Sentiment of Rationality," section 1, in *The Will to Believe: And Other Essays in Popular Philosophy* (1886).

6. Thomas Hobbes, *Leviathan*, part 1, chapter 6. Hobbes concluded that felicity or happiness is nothing more than "continual success in obtaining those things which a man from time to time desireth," one after another.

7. Henry D. Thoreau, "Economy," chapter 1, in *Walden*.

8. "It is impossible for any created good to constitute man's happiness. For happiness is the perfect good, which lulls the appetite altogether; else it would not be the last end, if something yet remained to be desired." Thomas Aquinas, *Summa Theologiae*, trans. Fathers of the English Dominican Province (1920), first part of the second part, question 2, article 8.

9. G. K. Chesterton, *Autobiography*, vol. 16 of *The Collected Works of G. K. Chesterton*, (San Francisco: Ignatius Press, 1988), 212.

10. As Thomas Aquinas argues, in the whole created universe we find only particular kinds of good that derive their goodness from something good in itself, which they reflect or in which they share. Therefore, the universal good at which all things aim must be outside the created universe. Aquinas, *Summa*, first part, question 103, article 2.

## Chapter 19: Is Happiness Something We Feel, We Have, or We Do?

1. Sean Kingston (Baby Bash), "What Is It," *Cyclone*, Arista Records, 2008, written by Ronald Bryant, J. R. Rotem, Marty James, Scott LaRock, and Lawrence Parker. I confess that Messrs. Kingston and Bash were not asking about the same "it" that we are.

## Chapter 20: If Happiness Is Something We Do, Then What Activity Is It?

1. My rendering of "Nam quaero ab omnibus, utrum malint de veritate quam de falsitate gaudere; tam non dubitant dicere de veritate se malle, quam non dubitant dicere beatos esse se velle. Beata quippe vita est gaudium de veritate." Augustine of Hippo, *Confessions*, book 10, chapter 26.

2. David Hume, *A Treatise of Human Nature* (1739–40), book 2, chapter 3, section 3.

3. John Keats, letter to Benjamin Bailey, November 22, 1817.

4. George Lucas, *Star Wars* (LucasFilm, 1977).

5. For additional discussion, see my *What We Can't Not Know: A Guide*, revised and expanded edition (San Francisco: Ignatius Press, 2011), 190–95.

6. Aristotle, *Metaphysics*, trans. W. D. Ross (1924), book 1, chapter 1.

## Chapter 21: Can We Do It on Our Own?

1. Psalm 88:12 (RSV-CE).

2. On the multiverse hypothesis one might, perhaps, imagine a process of natural selection in which the component universes are themselves the replicating things. But that would still leave the multiverse itself unexplained.

3. Peter Kreeft and Ronald K. Tacelli, "Twenty Arguments for the Existence of God" in *Handbook of Christian Apologetics* (Downers Grove, Illinois: InterVarsity Press, 1994).

4. For example, health is a created good, and disease is something amiss in health. It would be absurd to say that health is something amiss in disease, or that health and disease are entirely independent realities, each with its own nature.

5. I believe I owe both analogies to C. S. Lewis, but I have been unable to track them down.

6. Matthew 5:8 (KJV).

7. Augustine of Hippo, *Confessions*, trans. Frank J. Sheed, 2nd ed. (Indianapolis: Hackett, 2006), book 1, chapter 1.

8. G. K. Chesterton, *Orthodoxy* (1908), chapter 2.

## Chapter 22: Could We Ever Do It on Our Own?

1. Genesis 3:4–5 (RSV-CE).

2. See Genesis 2:9 and all of chapter 3 (RSV-CE).

3. Genesis 11. See, e.g., Augustine of Hippo, *The City of God against the Pagans*, trans. Marcus Dods, bk. 16, chapters 4–6, New Advent, www.newadvent.org/fathers.

4. Ibid., book 14, chapter 17.

5. The themes of disenchantment, "will to power," and the rise of the *übermensch* or superman are pervasive in Nietzsche's later work. See for example Friedrich Nietzsche, *Thus Spoke Zarathustra*, book 1, "Zarathustra's Prologue," sections 3–4.

6. Gary Marcus and Christof Koch, "The Plug-and-Play Brain," *Wall Street Journal*, March 15, 2014, published online as "The Future of Brain Implants," https://www.wsj.com/articles/SB10001424052702304914904579435592981780S

28. The authors borrow the quotation about faintheartedness from former president Ronald Reagan, who was not, of course, speaking of transhumanism.

7. See Mihail C. Roco and William Sims Bainbridge, eds., "Converging Technologies for Improving Human Performance: Nanotechnology, Biotechnology, Information Technology and Cognitive Science (also known as the NBIC Report), National Science Foundation and U.S. Department of Commerce, (2004), https://www.academia.edu/26151799/Converging_Tech nologies_for_Improving_Human_Performance.

8. *Morning Edition*, National Public Radio, January 7, 1998.

9. In several books, beginning with *The Physics of Immortality* (New York: Doubleday, 1994), Professor Tipler tries to prove that the laws of physics require the existence of God and the resurrection of the dead. What he means by these terms, however, is not what they mean in the Nicene Creed. He expects intelligent species to develop their scientific abilities at an exponentially increasing rate of growth, until eventually they evolve an unlimited intelligence that uses all of the resources of the universe. He identifies this intelligence with God. Because its computational speed will increase faster than the universe can collapse, in "experiential" terms its life will have infinite duration. This deathless intelligence will run simulations of every intelligent being that has ever existed. Consequently, all the dead will all live again forever in virtual reality, which will be indistinguishable from ordinary reality. Tipler considers the argument a confirmation of Christianity, a supposition about which, perhaps, nothing more need be said.

10. C. S. Lewis, *The Abolition of Man: Or Reflections on Education with Special Reference to the Teaching of English in the Upper Forms of Schools* (New York: Macmillan, 1947).

## Chapter 23: What Kind of Help Would We Need?

1. Alleged last words of Johann Wolfgang von Goethe. Attribution disputed.

2. 2 Peter 1:4 (RSV-CE).

3. 1 Corinthians 13:12 (RSV-CE).

4. I am relying on Thomas Aquinas's discussion in *Summa Theologiae*, trans. Fathers of the English Dominican Province (1920), first part of the second part, question 3, article 4, and question 4, article 3, which I discuss at greater length in J. Budziszewski, *Commentary on Thomas Aquinas's Treatise on Happiness and Ultimate Purpose* (Cambridge: Cambridge University Press, 2020).

5. 1 Corinthians 10:13 (RSV-CE).

## Chapter 24: How Can We Get That Help?

1.   1 Thessalonians 5:21a (RSV-CE).
2.   John Paul II, preface in *Fides et Ratio*, Vatican, http://www.vatican.va/content/john-paul-ii/en/encyclicals/documents/hf_jp-ii_enc_14091998_fides-et-ratio.html.
3.   Joseph Cardinal Ratzinger, *Introduction to Christianity* (New York: Herder and Herder, 1970), 94–95, 99.
4.   C. S. Lewis, *Perelandra* (New York: Macmillan, 1965), 201.

## Chapter 25: The Paradoxes of Perfect Fulfillment

1.   G. K. Chesterton, *Orthodoxy* (1908), chapter 6.
2.   Luke 9:23–24 and 17:33. Parallel passages can be found in all four Gospels; compare Matthew 10:39, Mark 8:34–35, and John 12:25.
3.   Bernadette Young, "Parenthood and Effective Altruism," Effective Altruism Forum, April 13, 2014, http://effective-altruism.com/ea/66/parenthood_and_effective_altruism.
4.   Janis Joplin, "Mercedes Benz," *Pearl*, Columbia, 1970, written by Janis Joplin, Michael McClure, and Bob Neuwirth.
5.   Psalm 34:18 (RSV-CE).
6.   Luke 6:20 (RSV-CE).
7.   Matthew 6:33 (RSV-CE).
8.   Augustine of Hippo, *Confessions*, trans. Frank J. Sheed, 2nd ed. (Indianapolis: Hackett, 2006), book 2, chapter 6, sections 13–14, pp. 31–32.
9.   Versions of the Beatitudes are given in both Matthew 5:1–12 and Luke 6:20–26.
10.  Matthew 5:8 (RSV-CE).
11.  2 Corinthians 5:4 (English Standard Version).

# Index

## A

Abbott and Costello, 19

absurdity, 11, 25–26, 77, 93, 199

accident, 128
 as luck, 120–22, 188
 contrasted with essence or
  nature, 26

activities
 as actualizations of
  potentialities, 158
 contrasted with feelings and
  conditions, 85–86, 149–56
 whether they always pass into
  things outside us, 151

Acton, John Emerich Edward
 Dalberg ["Lord Acton" in
 text], 75

Addison, Joseph, 34, 49, 58–61

Adler, Mortimer, 11

Aguilera, Christina, 67

Alcoholics Anonymous, 98

Alighieri, Dante, 82–83, 143

Al Qaeda, 101

angelism, 35–36

appetite, 17–18, 52, 82–83, 146n8,
 160
 cannot direct itself properly,
  77
 may conspire against reason,
  91–92
 rational, 8
 *See also* desire

aristocracy, 49

Aristotle, xvii, 4, 11n1, 20n3, 21,
 87, 101, 106n4, 112, 116n21, 123,
 138, 153, 163–64

Aquinas, Thomas, xvi, 15,
 68n28, 79n3, 105n3, 145–46,
 148n10, 186n4

Augustine of Hippo, 56–58,
 103n1, 115, 132–33, 138–39, 152,
 157n1, 163, 172, 176n3, 202–3

## B

Bach, Johann Sebastian, 131

Bainbridge, William Sims,
 180n7

Baumeister, Roy F., 65